DAY HIKES IN
YELLOWSTONE
NATIONAL PARK

54 GREAT HIKES

by Robert Stone

D0064033

Day Hike Books, Inc.

RED LODGE, MONTANA

Published by Day Hike Books, Inc.
P.O. Box 865
Red Lodge, Montana 59068

Distributed by The Globe Pequot Press
246 Goose Lane
P.O. Box 480
Guilford, CT 06437-0480
800-243-0495 (direct order) · 800-820-2329 (fax order)
www.globe-pequot.com

Photographs by Robert Stone
Design by Paula Doherty

The author has made every attempt to provide
accurate information in this book. The author and publisher do
not assume any responsibility for loss, damage or injury caused
through the use of this book. Please let this book guide you,
but be aware that each hiker assumes responsibility
for their own safety.

Cover photo: Lower Falls, Hike 19.
Back cover photo: Upper Geyser Basin, Hike 32.

Table of Contents

THE HIKES

Upper Yellowstone Park

Grand Canyon of the Yellowstone

Lower Yellowstone Park and Old Faithful

Yellowstone from the Gallatin

Around the Town of West Yellowstone

About the Hikes

Yellowstone National Park is a magnificent area with beautiful, dramatic scenery and incredible hydrothermal features. An extensive network of hiking trails weave through the mountains and valleys of the park. This guide will take you to 54 great day hikes, getting you to the trailhead and onto the trail with clear, concise directions.

Most of these hikes are within Yellowstone Park; a few are around the perimeter of the park. All of the trailheads can be easily accessed from the main roads. An overall map of the park and the hikes is found on pages 8—9.

These hikes have been chosen for their outstanding beauty, hydrothermal features, variety and ability to be hiked within the day. They include thundering waterfalls, geysers, hot springs, high mountain lakes, cascading rivers, meadows and panoramic views. These hikes will take you to incredible scenery and natural features found no where else on earth.

To help you decide which hikes are most appealing to you, a brief summary of the highlights is included with each hike. The hikes are also accompanied with their own maps and detailed driving and hiking directions. You may wish to enjoy these beautiful areas for the whole day.

Established as the world's first national park in 1872, Yellowstone has more than 150 waterfalls, numerous crystalline lakes, panoramic vistas and 1,200 miles of marked hiking trails lying within its 2.2 million acres. The wildlife includes moose, bison, grizzly and black bear, elk, deer, antelope, bighorn sheep, coyote, fox, wolf, beaver, otter, chipmunk, squirrel, marmot, trumpeter swan, white pelican, osprey, owl, bald eagle and much more. Every trip to Yellowstone will include a variety of animal and nature observations.

Sixty percent of the world's geysers are located in Yellowstone National Park, in addition to the more than 10,000 hot springs, bubbling mud pots and steaming fumaroles. There are over 150 geysers located in the Upper Geyser Basin alone, making it the greatest concentration of geysers in the world.

Old Faithful is located in this basin. The road to Old Faithful contains several other geyser basins as well. See your park map for locations of a few of these popular geothermal features.

Yellowstone Park also has hundreds of alpine lakes. Yellowstone Lake is North America's largest mountain lake. It is over 87,000 acres with one hundred miles of shoreline and an average depth of 139 feet.

The Yellowstone River flows out of this lake at its north end and soon roars down the magnificent Grand Canyon of the Yellowstone. This canyon is twenty miles long, spans 4,000 feet across and is 1,200 feet deep. The commanding Upper and Lower Falls are located within this canyon. Hikes can be found descending into the canyon and along its rim.

Most of the hikes listed in this guide are easy to moderately strenuous and are timed at a leisurely rate. To extend your hike farther into the backcountry, additional maps can be purchased at Yellowstone stores or sporting goods stores.

Be sure to wear supportive, comfortable hiking shoes and be prepared for inclement weather. The elevations range from 5,300 feet to 11,350 feet. At these altitudes, the air can be cool. Afternoon thundershowers are common throughout the summer. Wear layered clothing and bring a warm hat. A rain poncho, sunscreen, mosquito repellent, a snack and drinking water are highly recommended.

Hiking in Yellowstone will give you a deeper appreciation of the beauty of this region and will give you the opportunity to get away from the crowds. From one end of the park to the other, this area is rich in stunning landscape and diversity, waiting for you to discover it out on the trails.

NOTE: A bear bell is recommended to alert any bears in the area of your presence. Yellowstone has both black and grizzly bears. Surprising them is not safe. Hike with a friend or group if at all possible. The local ranger stations will have the latest information on bear activity in the areas you wish to hike.

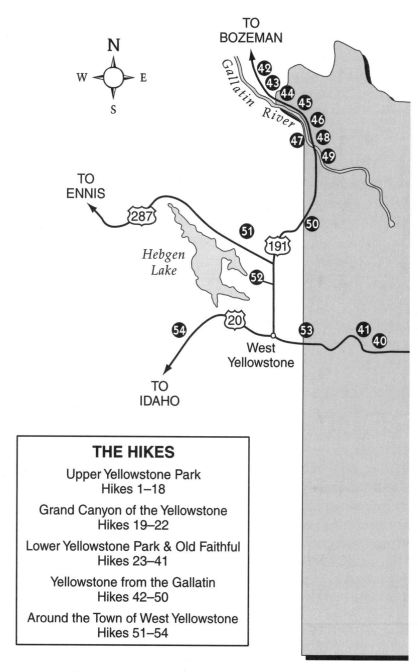

MAP OF THE HIKES

THE HIKES

Upper Yellowstone Park
Hikes 1–18

Grand Canyon of the Yellowstone
Hikes 19–22

Lower Yellowstone Park & Old Faithful
Hikes 23–41

Yellowstone from the Gallatin
Hikes 42–50

Around the Town of West Yellowstone
Hikes 51–54

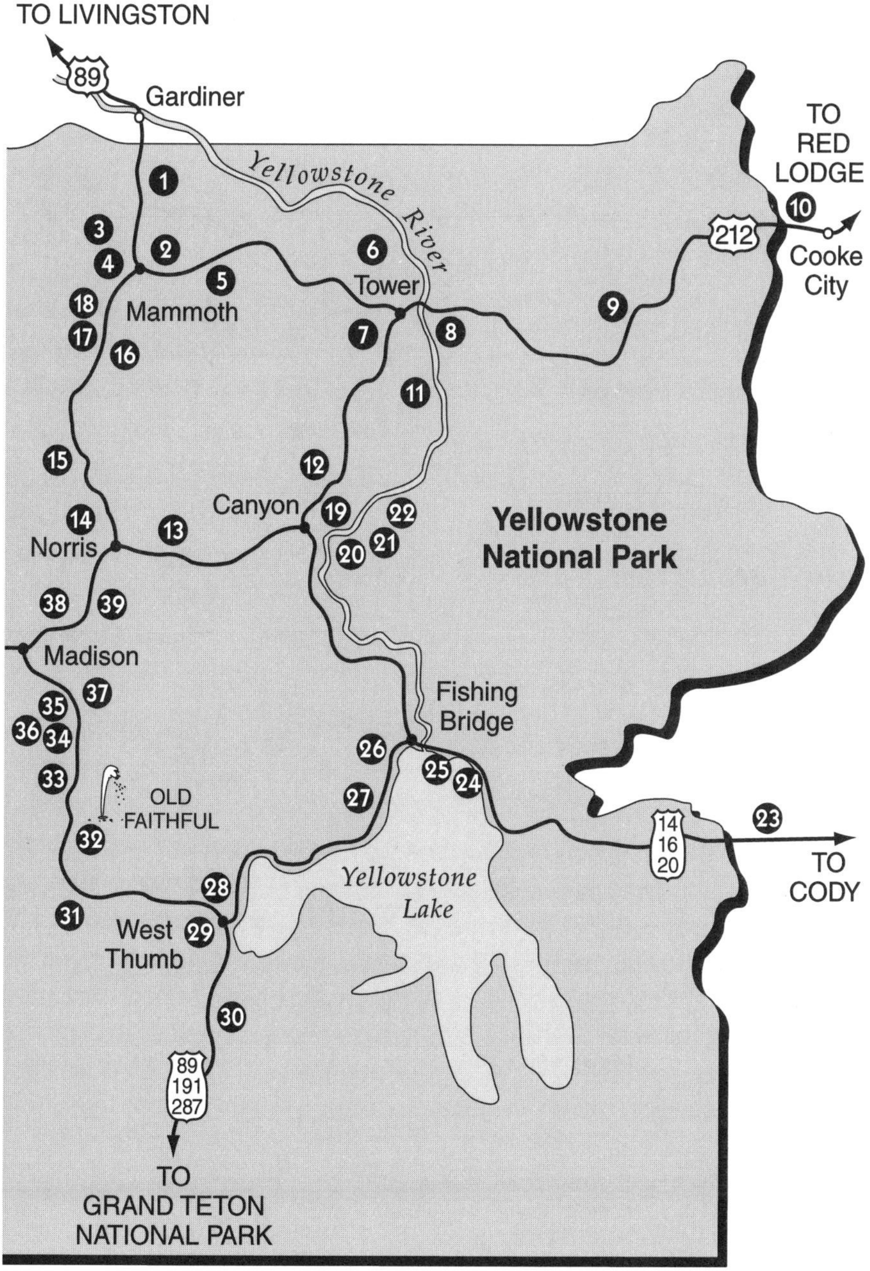

TO LIVINGSTON

89

Gardiner

Yellowstone River

TO RED LODGE

212

10

Cooke City

1

3

4

2

5

18

17

Mammoth

16

6

Tower

7

8

9

11

15

12

14

Norris

13

Canyon

19

22

20

21

Yellowstone National Park

38

39

Madison

35

37

36

34

33

32

OLD FAITHFUL

Fishing Bridge

26

25

24

27

Yellowstone Lake

31

West Thumb

28

29

30

89
191
287

TO CODY

14
16
20

23

TO GRAND TETON NATIONAL PARK

Hike 1
Boiling River Trail
and Swimming Hole

Hiking distance: 1 mile round trip
Hiking time: 40 minutes plus soaking
Elevation gain: Level
Maps: Trails Illustrated Mammoth Hot Springs
       U.S.G.S. Mammoth

Summary of hike: This hike is a popular and easy trail that clings to the west bank of the Gardner River en route to a hot springs. The hot springs flows over travertine rocks into the cool river, creating a swimming area with hot pools, small waterfalls and lush green vegetation. The river is heated from underground water from Mammoth Hot Springs. The trail lies on the 45th parallel, half way between the equator and the North Pole.

Driving directions: From the Mammoth Visitor Center, drive 2.3 miles north towards Gardiner to the sign which reads "45th Parallel of Latitude." Turn left or right and park in the lots on either side of the road.

Hiking directions: From the parking lot on the east side of the road, hike a half mile south on the level path. The trail heads upstream along the banks of the Gardner River on the well traveled path. The pools are easy to spot. Across the river are the rocky slopes of the McMinn Bench.

A longer hike to the pools begins from the Mammoth Campground and heads northeast, dropping 300 feet down to the river.

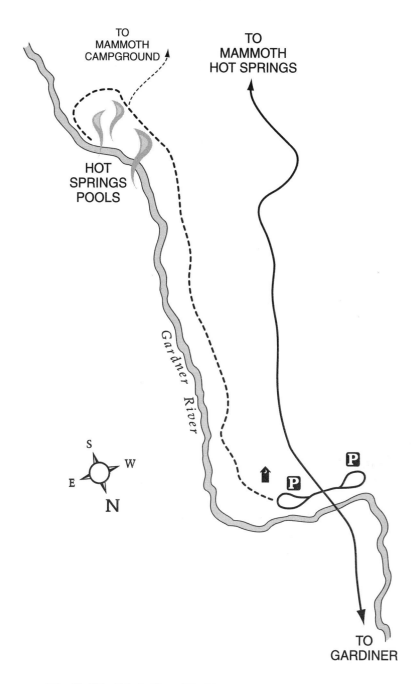

TO
MAMMOTH
CAMPGROUND

TO
MAMMOTH
HOT SPRINGS

HOT
SPRINGS
POOLS

Gardner River

S

W

E

N

P

P

TO
GARDINER

BOILING RIVER TRAIL

Hike 2
Lava Creek Trail to Undine Falls

Hiking distance: 6 miles round trip
Hiking time: 3 hours
Elevation gain: 500 feet
Maps: Trails Illustrated Mammoth Hot Springs
U.S.G.S. Mammoth

Summary of hike: This hike follows beside the Gardner River and Lava Creek up canyon to the dynamic Undine Falls. The waterfall drops 60 feet from the sheer volcanic canyon cliffs.

Driving directions: From the Mammoth Visitor Center, drive 0.9 miles to a road on the right with a sign which says "Residential Area." Turn right. Drive 0.2 miles, winding around a school to a road on the left with a sign that says "service road." Continue on the left road 0.6 miles to the trailhead pullout on the right.

Hiking directions: From the parking pullout, the trail leads toward the Gardner River. It winds around the hill to a bridge crossing the river. After crossing, continue to the right, following the river upstream. The trail will leave the Gardner River and begin following Lava Creek. As you near Undine Falls, the trail climbs to the top of the cliffs for a tremendous view of the falls. There are log crossings past the falls that lead to the Undine Falls Overlook on the other side. Many hikers cross the logs, but it is not advisable. It can be dangerous. To return, take the same trail down the canyon back to the parking pullout.

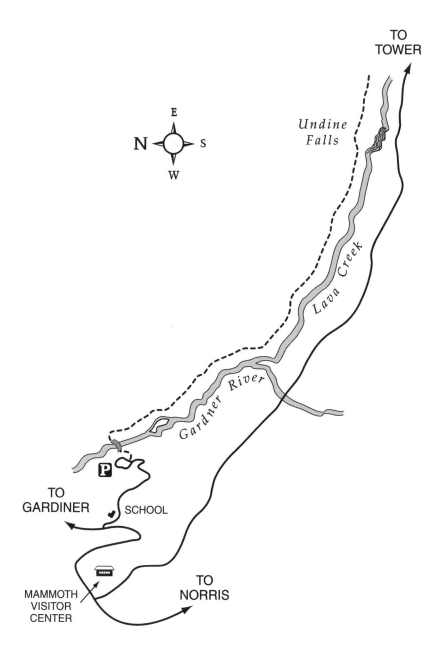

LAVA CREEK
TO UNDINE FALLS

Hike 3
Beaver Ponds Loop

Hiking distance: 5 mile loop
Hiking time: 2.5 hours
Elevation gain: 550 feet
Maps: Trails Illustrated Mammoth Hot Springs
U.S.G.S. Mammoth

Summary of hike: The Beaver Ponds Loop begins by climb-ing up Clematis Gulch through a shady spruce and fir forest, gaining 350 feet in the first half mile. The trail then traverses rolling hills, connecting forests, meadows, scenic overlooks and a series of beaver ponds.

Driving directions: From the Mammoth Visitor Center, drive 0.3 miles towards Norris to the Mammoth Hot Springs Lower Terraces. Park in the lots on either side of the road.

Hiking directions: The trailhead is on the north side of the Mammoth Terraces by the bus parking lot next to Clematis Creek. Hike west between Liberty Cap and the stone house, crossing a footbridge over the creek. Head up Clematis Gulch to a junction. Take the right fork, recrossing Clematis Creek and continuing up the gulch. At 0.7 miles, the trail curves north to a signed junction with the Sepulcher Ridge Trail. Go right on the Beaver Ponds Trail to a ridge overlooking Mam-moth, Sheep Mountain and Mount Everts. Continue north along the ridge, ducking in and out of the forest and across a wooden bridge. At 2.4 miles the trail descends to the first pond. After the third pond, the trail crosses four bridges and several streams. At the north end of the trail, follow a stream through grassy meadows, and head south along the shoreline of a large pond. Cross the outlet stream by a beaver dam, and weave through the forest to a plateau covered in sage-brush. Return along the plateau, and descend back down into Mammoth by the hotel.

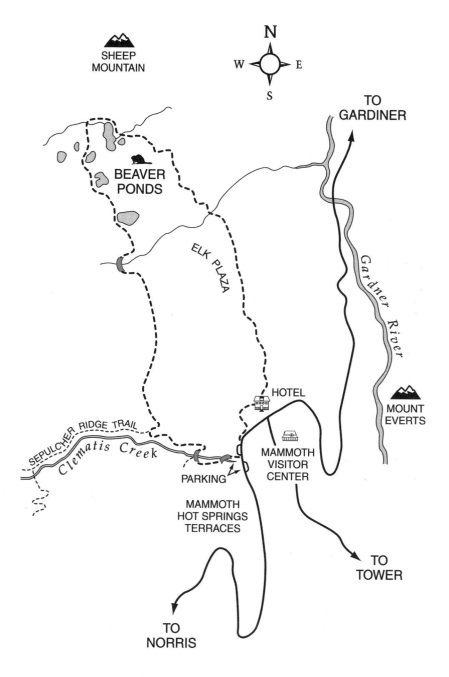

SHEEP MOUNTAIN

N
W   E
S

TO GARDINER

BEAVER PONDS

ELK PLAZA

Gardner River

HOTEL

MOUNT EVERTS

SEPULCHER RIDGE TRAIL

Clematis Creek

MAMMOTH VISITOR CENTER

PARKING

MAMMOTH HOT SPRINGS TERRACES

TO TOWER

TO NORRIS

BEAVER PONDS LOOP

Hike 4
Mammoth Hot Springs
Terrace Trails

Hiking distance: 1 mile round trip
Hiking time: 1 hour
Elevation gain: 300 feet
Maps: Trails Illustrated Mammoth Hot Springs
Yellowstone Association Mammoth Hot Springs map
U.S.G.S. Mammoth

Summary of hike: This hike is a series of walkway and boardwalk loops. They lead through magnificent travertine terraces formed by mineral laden hot water, limestone and carbon dioxide. The many colors of these terraces are from living bacteria and algae. These colors change at different temperatures. White and yellow are the hottest. As the water cools, brown, green and orange algae take hold. The mineral formations are shaped by flowing water from the springs and ground slope. These landscapes are in constant evolving motion. If you have an opportunity to visit in the winter, you will witness these hot springs at their best.

Driving directions: From the Mammoth Visitor Center, drive 0.3 miles on the Grand Loop Road towards Norris. The terraces are easily visible. There are parking lots located on both sides of the road.

Hiking directions: From the parking lot, hike towards Liberty Cap, an extinct hot spring cone that stands out like a giant monolith at the start of the trail. There are various routes to take. They all loop around and interconnect throughout the lower terraces. Choose your own route. Be sure to drive the upper terrace loop, which enters a forested area. During the winter this road is a wonderful cross-country ski trail.

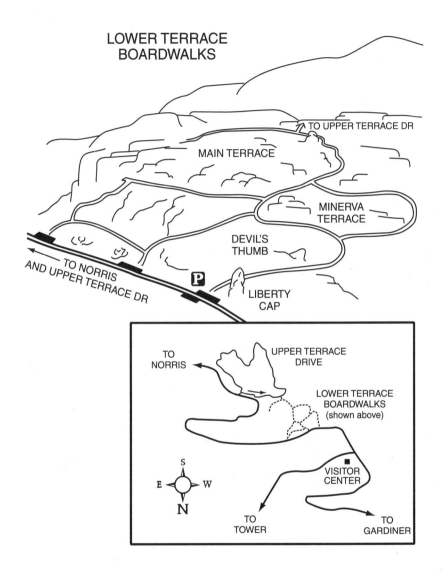

MAMMOTH HOT SPRINGS TERRACE TRAILS

Hike 5
Wraith Falls

Hiking distance: 1 mile round trip
Hiking time: 30 minutes
Elevation gain: Level
Maps: Trails Illustrated Mammoth Hot Springs
U.S.G.S. Blacktail Deer Creek

Summary of hike: The trail to Wraith Falls is a short, easy and beautiful hike. Along the way, the trail crosses a footbridge over Lupine Creek. Although Wraith Falls looks like a waterfall, smells like a waterfall and is called a waterfall, it is actually an 80-foot cascade down an inclined rock in Lupine Creek. The forested area has spruce, lodgepole pine and Douglas fir trees.

Driving directions: From Mammoth, drive 5 miles southeast towards Tower to the Wraith Falls parking area on the right. It is located 0.4 miles past the Lava Creek picnic area.

From Tower Junction, drive 13 miles northwest towards Mammoth to the Wraith Falls parking area on the left.

Hiking directions: From the parking area, follow the well-marked trail south. The path has two short boardwalks that protect the fragile plant life in the open meadows. The trail ends at a wooden observation platform 100 yards in front of Wraith Falls. Return along the same trail back to the parking area.

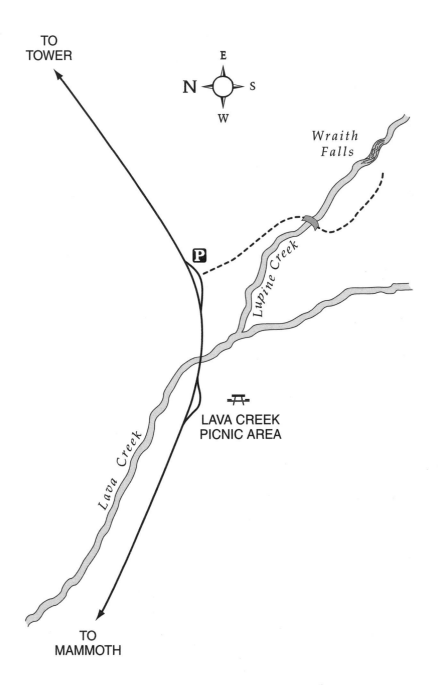

TO
TOWER

E
N
S
W

*Wraith
Falls*

P

Lupine Creek

Lava Creek

🔥 LAVA CREEK
PICNIC AREA

TO
MAMMOTH

WRAITH FALLS

Hike 6
Hellroaring Creek

Hiking distance: 4 miles round trip
Hiking time: 2 hours
Elevation gain: 700 feet
Maps: Trails Illustrated Tower/Canyon
      U.S.G.S. Tower Junction

Summary of hike: Hellroaring Creek is a wide rocky creek that flows into the Yellowstone River. At the creek, you can see Hellroaring Mountain to the north and Buffalo Plateau to the east. The hike crosses a metal suspension bridge high above the turbulent water of the Yellowstone River in a steep and narrow canyon. Hellroaring Creek also offers excellent trout fishing.

Driving directions: From Tower Junction, drive 3.7 miles northwest towards Mammoth to the signed Hellroaring trailhead turnoff and turn right. Continue 0.2 miles on the unpaved road to the parking area at the road's end.

From Mammoth, drive 14.5 miles southeast towards Tower Junction to the Hellroaring trailhead turnoff and turn left.

Hiking directions: Head northeast across the rolling hills. Switchbacks lead down towards the Black Canyon of the Yellowstone. At 0.8 miles, a trail leading to Tower intersects from the right. Continue straight ahead to the sturdy suspension bridge crossing the surging Yellowstone River in a deep gorge. After crossing, head north through the forested draw to a junction with the Buffalo Plateau Trail at 1.5 miles. Continue north across the sagebrush hills, reaching a pond and a trail split at two miles. The left fork circles the pond to Hellroaring Creek. Across the creek, the Yellowstone River Trail leads to Gardiner. The right fork heads upstream to a patrol cabin at just under a mile and a stock bridge shortly after. Return by retracing your route.

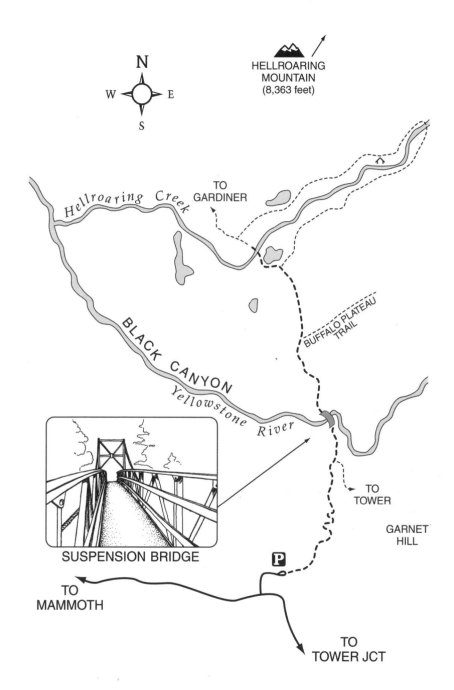

N
W E
S

HELLROARING
MOUNTAIN
(8,363 feet)

Hellroaring Creek

TO
GARDINER

BUFFALO PLATEAU
TRAIL

BLACK CANYON

Yellowstone River

SUSPENSION BRIDGE

TO
TOWER

GARNET
HILL

P

TO
MAMMOTH

TO
TOWER JCT

HELLROARING CREEK

Hike 7
Lost Lake and Lost Creek Falls

Hiking distance: 4 miles round trip
Hiking time: 2 hours
Elevation gain: 450 feet
Maps: Trails Illustrated Tower/Canyon
  U.S.G.S. Tower Junction

Summary of hike: This hike has views of the 40-foot Lost Creek Falls from the base of the falls and again from the top overlooking the falls. The hike also takes you to Lost Lake—a long, narrow six-acre lake that has yellow water lilies and is frequented by ducks. This beautiful area is bordered by forested hillsides on both ends of the lake.

Driving directions: The trailhead is at Roosevelt Lodge, located at Tower Junction. Park in the west side of the parking lot near the lodge.

Hiking directions: From the parking area, walk to the back of Roosevelt Lodge. The trailhead is directly behind the lodge and is easy to spot. There are two trails. To begin, take the left trail 0.2 miles to a magnificent view of Lost Creek Falls from its base. This short trail is surrounded by steep canyon cliffs. Return to the trailhead, and now take the right fork towards Lost Lake, which immediately crosses a footbridge over Lost Creek. Continue through this forested area 0.6 miles to a trail junction. The right trail goes to Lost Lake. First, take the left fork 0.6 miles to an overlook of Lost Creek Falls. Although this trail continues to Tower Falls, this hike returns 0.6 miles back to the trail junction. This time, take the right fork (west) 0.2 miles to Lost Lake. The trail follows the north shore of the lake. To return, take the same trail back to Roosevelt Lodge.

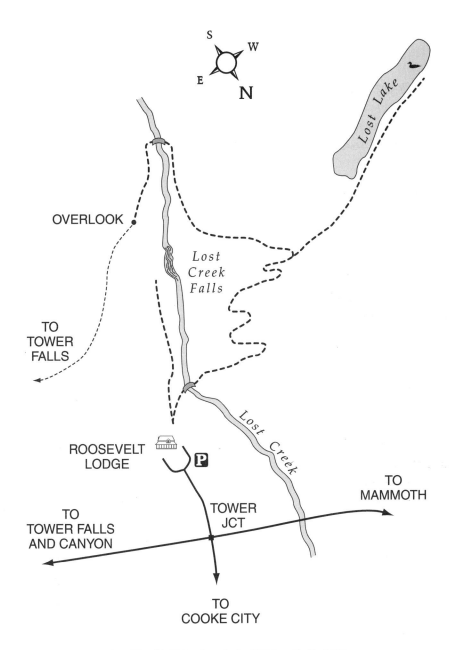

S W E N (compass)

Lost Lake

OVERLOOK •

Lost Creek Falls

TO TOWER FALLS

Lost Creek

ROOSEVELT LODGE 🏠 P

TO TOWER FALLS AND CANYON

TOWER JCT

TO MAMMOTH

TO COOKE CITY

LOST LAKE AND LOST CREEK FALLS

Hike 8
Yellowstone River Picnic Area Trail

Hiking distance: 4 miles round trip
Hiking time: 2 hours
Elevation gain: 300 feet
Maps: Trails Illustrated Tower/Canyon
      U.S.G.S. Tower Junction

Summary of hike: This easy hike parallels the Grand Canyon of the Yellowstone and the Yellowstone River along the eastern edge of the canyon rim. From 700 feet above the river, the hike offers continuous views of eroded rock formations, including Bumpus Butte, The Needle, The Narrows, Overhanging Cliff, Devil's Den and the towers at Tower Falls.

Driving directions: From Tower Junction, drive 1.2 miles northeast towards Cooke City to the Yellowstone River Picnic Area on the right.

Hiking directions: The signed trail begins on the east side of the picnic area. Head south, gaining 200 feet up the grassy hillside to the ridge. From the ridge are views across the canyon and down to the Yellowstone River. From here, the trail levels out and continues southeast along the ridge. At 1.5 miles, the canyon and trail curve left. The trail crosses the plateau and connects with the Specimen Ridge Trail heading east and the Bannock Indian Trail dropping south into the canyon and down to the river. This junction is a good stopping place. Return to the trailhead along the same trail.

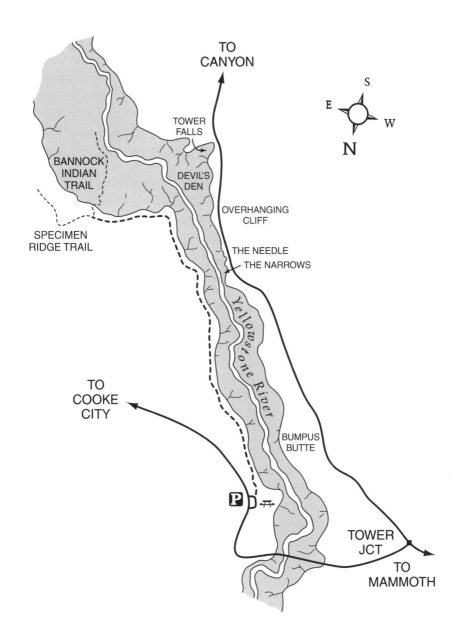

TO
CANYON

S

E   W

N

TOWER
FALLS

DEVIL'S
DEN

BANNOCK
INDIAN
TRAIL

OVERHANGING
CLIFF

SPECIMEN
RIDGE TRAIL

THE NEEDLE
THE NARROWS

Yellowstone River

TO
COOKE
CITY

BUMPUS
BUTTE

P

TOWER
JCT

TO
MAMMOTH

YELLOWSTONE RIVER
PICNIC AREA TRAIL

Hike 9
Trout Lake

Hiking distance: 2.2 miles round trip
Hiking time: 1 hour
Elevation gain: 200 feet
Maps: Trails Illustrated Tower/Canyon
      U.S.G.S. Abiathar Peak and Mount Hornaday

Summary of hike: Trout Lake, a great rainbow trout fishing lake, sits in a beautiful bowl. The round, twelve-acre lake is surrounded by rolling meadows, Douglas fir and lodgepole pine forests, and a sheer rock mountain wall to the north. From the lake are views of Mount Hornaday, The Thunderer, Druid Peak and Frederick Peak.

Driving directions: From Tower Junction, drive 17.8 miles northeast towards Cooke City to the unmarked trailhead pullout on the left. The pullout is 1.2 miles southwest of the Pebble Creek Campground.

Hiking directions: From the parking pullout, hike west past the trail sign towards the forest. Begin ascending the hillside to the forested ridge. Along the way, the cascading outlet stream of Trout Lake tumbles down the drainage to the left of the trail. At 0.6 miles, the trail reaches the southeast corner of Trout Lake at the outlet. Cross the log bridge over the creek. Once across, the trail follows the forested shoreline. A short distance ahead, the trail leaves the forest and heads into open, rolling meadows. Continue along the shoreline, circling the lake back to the junction by the outlet stream. Take the left fork, returning to the trailhead.

DRUID PEAK
(9,584 feet)

FREDERICK
PEAK
(9,422 feet)

TO
TOWER
JCT

*Trout
Lake*

MOUNT
HORNADAY
(7,435 feet)

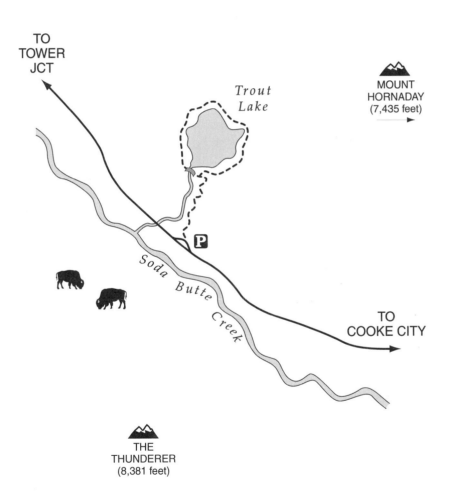

P

Soda Butte Creek

TO
COOKE CITY

THE
THUNDERER
(8,381 feet)

TROUT LAKE

Hike 10
Silver Falls

Hiking distance: 2 miles round trip
Hiking time: 1 hour
Elevation gain: 350 feet
Maps: Rocky Mountain Survey—Cooke City
      U.S.G.S. Cooke City

Summary of hike: Silver Falls is a narrow but long waterfall with a drop of more than 100 feet. The hike to the falls is located along the eastern border of Yellowstone National Park. There is no trail to the falls. It is a scramble over and around down trees parallel to Silver Creek. The terrain is rough and not recommended for children.

Driving directions: From the northeast entrance station of Yellowstone National Park, drive 0.5 miles east (outside the park) to the old road on the left on the west side of Silver Creek. Turn left and park. You may also park on Highway 212, a hundred yards back, in a car pullout on the north side of the road. The pullout is next to the Yellowstone National Park border sign. From Silvergate, the turnoff is located 0.6 miles west on Highway 212.

Hiking directions: From either parking area, walk back to Silver Creek. Follow the creek upstream along its west side. There is no trail and there are many down trees to navigate around. Continue to follow the creek, which leads to the falls. The last quarter mile is a steep climb up a knoll, leaving the creek below. At the top is a view across the canyon of Silver Falls.

There is also a second route to view the falls. Instead of climbing the knoll, stay close to Silver Creek in the canyon. This route will take you to the base of the falls.

From either route, return by following the creek downstream.

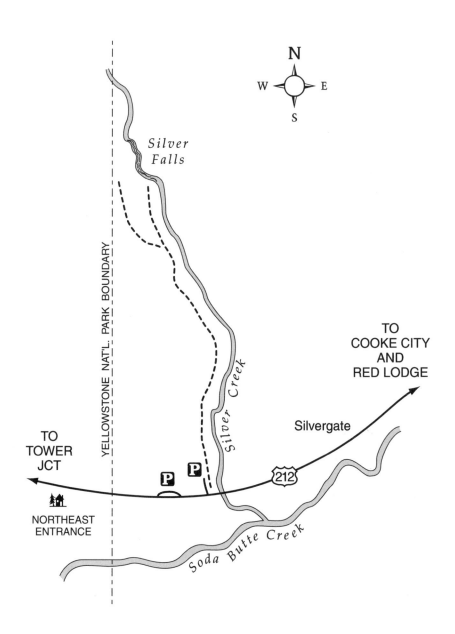

SILVER FALLS

Hike 11
Tower Falls and the
Yellowstone River Trail

Hiking distance: 3 miles round trip
Hiking time: 2 hours
Elevation gain: 300 feet
Maps: Trails Illustrated Tower/Canyon
U.S.G.S. Tower Junction

Summary of hike: This hike offers a walk along the Yellowstone River with the tall, steep walls of the Grand Canyon of the Yellowstone on each side. En route to the river are two separate locations to view Tower Falls. The first view is from an overlook along the trail. The other is from the base of this 130-foot falls with its volcanic pinnacles towering above.

Driving directions: The Tower Falls parking lot is 2.4 miles south of Tower Junction and 16.5 miles north of Canyon Junction. There is a general store on the east side of the road near the parking lot.

Hiking directions: From the parking lot, walk towards the general store. The trailhead is clearly visible along the right side of the store. A short distance from here is the overlook of Tower Falls. Continue down into the canyon to a trail junction. The best view of the falls is to the left. It is here, at the base of the falls, that a man was heard to exclaim, "This is the place to see it from, Phyllis!"

After viewing the falls, return to the junction. Now take the left fork downhill to the Yellowstone River. Continue up river to the right. This trail continues into the Grand Canyon of the Yellowstone. The open area along this portion of the canyon encourages off-trail exploring. Return on the same trail back to the Tower Falls parking lot.

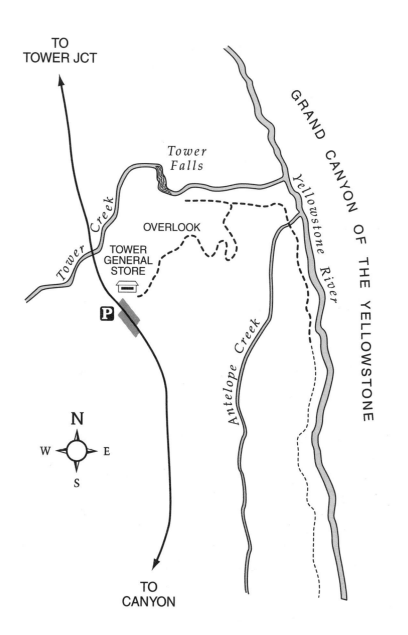

TO
TOWER JCT

GRAND CANYON OF THE YELLOWSTONE

Tower Falls

Yellowstone River

Tower Creek

OVERLOOK

TOWER
GENERAL
STORE

P

Antelope Creek

N
W E
S

TO
CANYON

TOWER FALLS
AND THE
YELLOWSTONE RIVER TRAIL

Hike 12
Cascade Lake Trail

Hiking distance: 5 miles round trip
Hiking time: 2.5 hours
Elevation gain: Level
Maps: Trails Illustrated Mammoth Hot Springs
      and Tower/Canyon
      U.S.G.S. Cook Peak and Mount Washburn

Summary of hike: The Cascade Lake Trail is a level hike to the shores of Cascade Lake. The trail leads through large open meadows, stands of lodgepole pine trees, and across many streams and footbridges. Part of the hike follows alongside Cascade Creek. With wildflowers covering the meadows and the mountains in the distance, this is a magical and favorite hike.

Driving directions: From Canyon Junction, drive 1.3 miles north towards Tower to the Cascade Lake Picnic Area on the left. Turn left and park in any picnic pullout area.

Hiking directions: The trailhead is on the south end of the Cascade Lake Picnic Area. The well-defined trail gently winds through the open meadows while crossing numerous streams. Cascade Lake is at the far end of the meadow. To return, take the same trail back.

There is another trail to Cascade Lake—the Cascade Creek Trail. This trailhead is located 0.5 miles west of Canyon Junction. The Cascade Lake Trail and the Cascade Creek Trail join in the meadow about one mile east of Cascade Lake. Although both trails are similar in distance, the Cascade Creek Trail is subject to heavy horse use.

Moose and grizzly bear can be spotted in this area. Always check with the rangers about bear activity before heading into the backcountry.

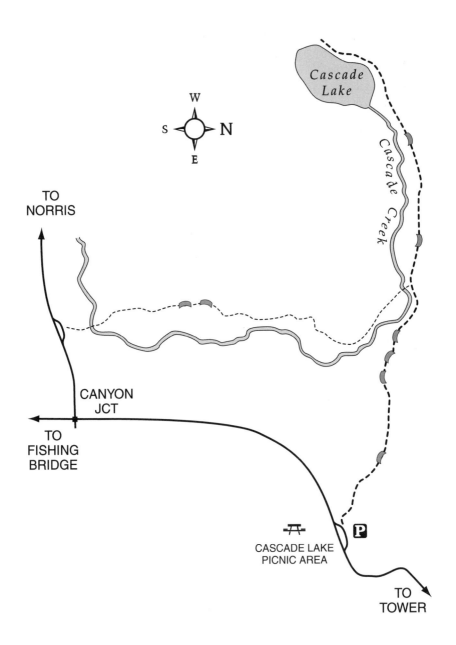

CASCADE LAKE TRAIL

Hike 13
Ice Lake and Little Gibbon Falls Loop

Hiking distance: 4.5 mile loop
Hiking time: 2 hours
Elevation gain: 150 feet
Maps: Trails Illustrated Mammoth Hot Springs
　　　　U.S.G.S. Norris Junction and Crystal Falls

Summary of hike: The Ice Lake Loop is an easy, incredibly diverse and lightly used hiking trail. The trail leads to a large and deep lake, a stunning 25-foot waterfall, a canyon with a cascading river, several river crossings and a pastoral meadow along the meandering Gibbon River. Part of the trail leads through a burn area from the 1988 fires. This area is blanketed with a new forest of small pine trees.

Driving directions: The Ice Lake trailhead parking area is located 8.2 miles west of Canyon Junction and 3.4 miles east of Norris Junction. The turnout is on the north side of the road.

Hiking directions: From the parking pullout, the trail heads north across a wooden bridge into the lodgepole pine forest. There is a trail split a short distance ahead. Bear to the left, along the west side of Ice Lake, to a junction with the Howard Eaton Trail. Take the right fork along the north shore of the lake. Continue past the lake to a crossing of the Gibbon River. Downfall logs can be used to cross. At 2.3 miles is a junction with the Wolf Lake Trail. Take the right fork towards Little Gibbon Falls. As you approach the cascading Gibbon River, the trail descends to a small canyon. Use a log to cross the river and climb the ridge to an overlook of Little Gibbon Falls. The trail follows the canyon and river southwest into Virginia Meadows. Hike through the meadows and back to the highway 0.5 miles east of the trailhead. Follow the road to the right, completing the loop.

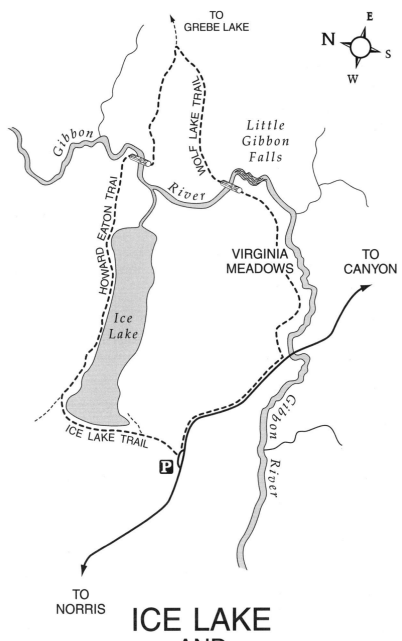

TO
GREBE LAKE

N E W S

Gibbon

WOLF LAKE TRAIL

*Little
Gibbon
Falls*

HOWARD EATON TRAIL

River

*Ice
Lake*

VIRGINIA
MEADOWS

TO
CANYON

*Gibbon
River*

ICE LAKE TRAIL

P

TO
NORRIS

ICE LAKE
AND
LITTLE GIBBON FALLS

Hike 14
Norris Geyser Basin

Hiking distance: 1.8 mile double loop
Hiking time: 1.5 hours
Elevation gain: 100 feet
Maps: Trails Illustrated Mammoth Hot Springs
Yellowstone Association Norris Geyser Basin map
U.S.G.S. Norris Junction

Summary of hike: Norris Geyser Basin is the hottest geyser basin in Yellowstone. The highly acidic water has created a stark, barren landscape. The geyser basin has two main loops—the Back Basin Trail and the Porcelain Basin Trail. Both loops begin and end at the museum. From the museum, there is an overlook of Porcelain Basin.

Driving directions: From Norris Junction, drive 0.4 miles west on the Norris Geyser Basin Road to the parking lot at the end of the road.

Hiking directions: Hike west on the paved path to the bookstore and museum. From the museum, take the left fork, heading south on the Back Basin Trail. Head left across a series of wooden walkways and overlooks to a trail split. The right fork is a cut-across for a shorter loop. The left fork leads to viewing platforms for Echinus Geyser, which erupts every 35 to 75 minutes. The trail continues past a variety of geysers and caldrons, returning to the west side of the museum at an overlook. Begin the loop around Porcelain Basin on the left fork, heading downhill into the pine forest. The trail crosses the stark but colorful basin on a wooden boardwalk. After looping through the basin, take the left fork at a junction up to the Porcelain Terrace Overlook. From the overlook, the trail curves to the right, completing the loop back at the museum.

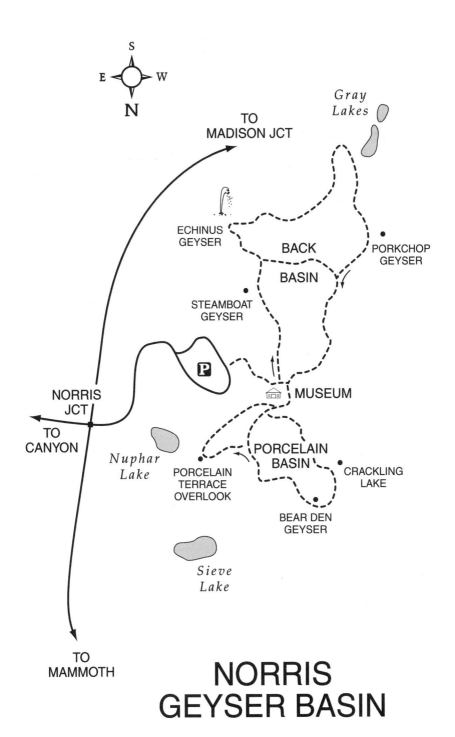

S

E ⊕ W

N

TO
MADISON JCT

*Gray
Lakes*

ECHINUS
GEYSER

BACK

PORKCHOP
GEYSER

BASIN

STEAMBOAT
GEYSER

P

NORRIS
JCT

TO
CANYON

*Nuphar
Lake*

MUSEUM

PORCELAIN
BASIN

PORCELAIN
TERRACE
OVERLOOK

CRACKLING
LAKE

BEAR DEN
GEYSER

*Sieve
Lake*

TO
MAMMOTH

NORRIS
GEYSER BASIN

Hike 15
Grizzly Lake

Hiking distance: 3.6 miles round trip
Hiking time: 2 hours
Elevation gain: 400 feet
Maps: Trails Illustrated Mammoth Hot Springs
      U.S.G.S. Obsidian Cliff and Mount Holmes

Summary of hike: Grizzly Lake, a 140-acre lake, sits in a narrow valley between two ridges. Before dropping down into the valley, the trail leads to a ridge above the lake. From this ridge is a great overlook with views of Mount Holmes, Trilobite Point, Dome Mountain and Antler Peak. The trail leads through a burned area from the 1976 and 1988 fires. It is fascinating to see the new growth of the future forest.

Driving directions: From Norris Junction, drive 6.2 miles north towards Mammoth to a signed parking pullout on the left.
    From Mammoth, drive 14.8 miles south towards Norris to the signed parking pullout on the right.

Hiking directions: The trail heads north, parallel to the road for a short distance. Cross a wooden bridge over Obsidian Creek and wind through the open meadow, crossing two more bridges en route. At the west end of the meadow, switchbacks lead 250 feet up the hill. From the ridge, traverse the hillside up the draw. Beyond the draw, the trail crosses a series of meadows and rolling hills to an overlook at 1.4 miles. Begin a switchbacking descent, dropping 300 feet to the north end of Grizzly Lake. Continue around the tip of the lake to Straight Creek, the inlet stream of the lake. Though the trail continues, this is the turnaround point for the hike. Follow the same path back.

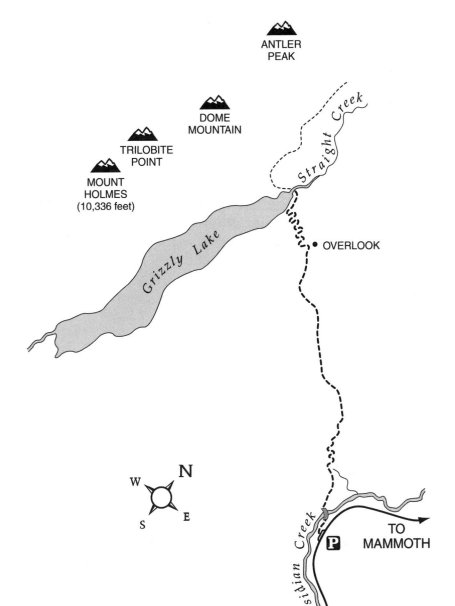

ANTLER
PEAK

DOME
MOUNTAIN

TRILOBITE
POINT

MOUNT
HOLMES
(10,336 feet)

Straight Creek

Grizzly Lake

OVERLOOK

N
W   E
S

Obsidian Creek

P

TO
MAMMOTH

TO
NORRIS

GRIZZLY
LAKE

Hike 16
Bunsen Peak

Hiking distance: 4.4 miles round trip
Hiking time: 2 hours
Elevation gain: 1,345 feet
Maps: Trails Illustrated Mammoth Hot Springs
U.S.G.S. Mammoth

Summary of hike: Dome-shaped Bunsen Peak is the eroded remains of a volcanic cone. From the top of Bunsen Peak are incredible views. You can see Mount Holmes to the southwest; Gardners Hole, the Gallatin Range and Electric Peak to the west; Cathedral Rock, the Mammoth Terraces and the Absaroka Range to the north; and the Washburn Range to the east. The trail to the peak winds through a burned Douglas fir and lodgepole pine forest from the 1988 fires. A beautiful new-growth forest has carpeted the hillsides.

Driving directions: From Mammoth, drive 4.7 miles south to the Glen Creek Trailhead parking lot on the left, just after crossing Golden Gate Bridge. From Norris Junction, drive 16.2 miles north towards Mammoth to the Glen Creek Trailhead parking lot on the right.

Hiking directions: Walk twenty yards up the gated, unpaved Bunsen Peak Road to the signed Bunsen Peak Trail on the left. Head northeast on the footpath, winding up the hillside while viewing Bunsen Peak to the east. The trail levels out through a burned area, then climbs a slope to a saddle. Views open up of Gardners Hole, Swan Lake and the Gallatin Range to the south and west. Begin the steep ascent to the peak. A short distance ahead, switchbacks zigzag up the west slope of the mountain, minimizing the steep grade. Near the top, the trail passes radio relay equipment and heads south to the peak. Return along the same path.

To hike further, the trail continues east down the mountain and joins Bunsen Peak Road, one mile from Osprey Falls.

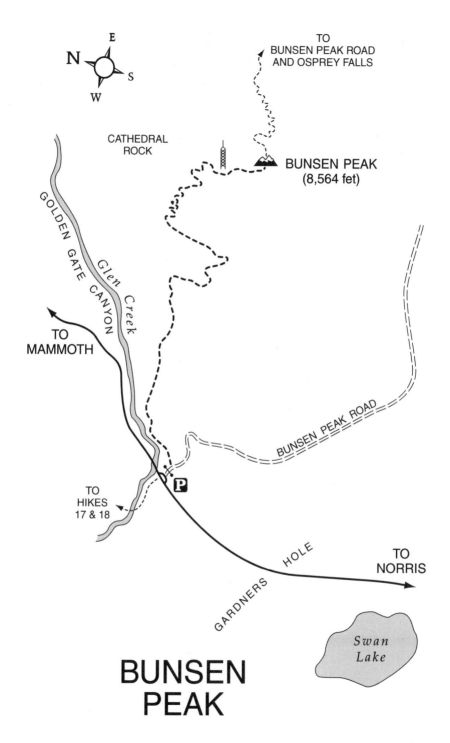

N E S W

TO
BUNSEN PEAK ROAD
AND OSPREY FALLS

CATHEDRAL
ROCK

BUNSEN PEAK
(8,564 fet)

GOLDEN GATE CANYON

Glen Creek

TO
MAMMOTH

BUNSEN PEAK ROAD

TO
HIKES
17 & 18

P

GARDNERS HOLE

TO
NORRIS

Swan
Lake

BUNSEN
PEAK

Hike 17
The Hoodoos

Hiking distance: 3 miles round trip
Hiking time: 1.5 hours
Elevation gain: 400 feet
Maps: Trails Illustrated Mammoth Hot Springs
       U.S.G.S. Mammoth

Summary of hike: The Hoodoos are odd shaped travertine formations standing like statues in a large rock garden. The sculpted rocks were formed by ancient hot spring deposits on Terrace Mountain, then tumbled down in a large landslide. This hike follows the eastern slope of Terrace Mountain to the Hoodoos.

Driving directions: The Hoodoos are located on the road between Mammoth and Norris. From Mammoth, drive 4.7 miles south to the Glen Creek Trailhead parking lot on the left, just after crossing Golden Gate Bridge. From Norris Junction, drive 16.2 miles north towards Mammoth to the Glen Creek Trailhead parking lot on the right.

Hiking directions: Cross the park road and take the signed Glen Creek Trail west across the grassy meadow. Cross a wooden bridge over the meandering Glen Creek to a signed junction at 0.2 miles. Take the Howard Eaton Trail to the right through the forested terrain and up to a ridge. Traverse the cliffside along the east edge of Terrace Mountain, heading north. At 1.3 miles the path enters the Hoodoos. Stroll through this incredible display of rocks to the end of the formations. This is our turnaround spot. Return by retracing your route.

    To hike further, the Howard Eaton Trail continues to Mammoth, or you may circle Terrace Mountain through Snow Pass (Hike 18).

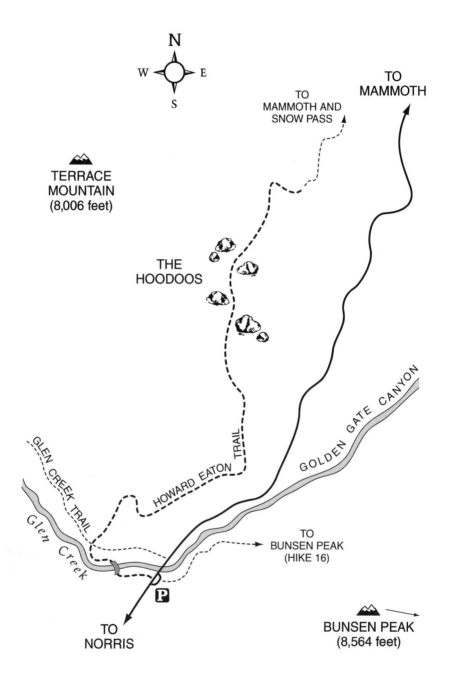

THE HOODOOS

Hike 18
Terrace Mountain Loop

Hiking distance: 6.2 mile loop
Hiking time: 3 hours
Elevation gain: 600 feet
Maps: Trails Illustrated Mammoth Hot Springs
U.S.G.S. Mammoth

Summary of hike: The Terrace Mountain Loop literally circles Terrace Mountain. The hike weaves through the Hoodoos, a garden of dynamic travertine rock formations (Hike 17). The northern part of the hike crosses Pinyon Terrace and Snow Pass between Terrace Mountain and Clagett Butte. The return route follows Glen Creek through Gardners Hole.

Driving directions: Follow the driving directions for Hike 17 to the Glen Creek Trailhead parking lot.

Hiking directions: Cross the park road, picking up the signed Glen Creek Trail. Cross the meadow to a signed junction at 0.2 miles. Bear right on the Howard Eaton Trail through the forested terrain, curving east to a ridge directly across from Bunsen Peak. Head north, following the cliffside through the Hoodoos, a dramatic garden of travertine boulders. Past the formations, follow the rolling hills through meadows, aspens and pine groves to a signed junction at 2.6 miles. Take the trail to the left towards Snow Pass. Watch for a deep fissure on the left 0.3 miles from the junction. Cross Pinyon Terrace, passing a junction with the Clagett Butte Trail on the right. Continue west through Snow Pass along the base of Clagett Butte, parallel to power poles. Cross the narrow pass past a kidney-shaped pond on the left tucked into a bowl. Curve around the pond to a saddle and descend along the north edge of the meadow. Cross under the power lines and bear left on a double-track trail. Head south along the west edge of Terrace Mountain, returning through the valley on the Glen Creek Trail.

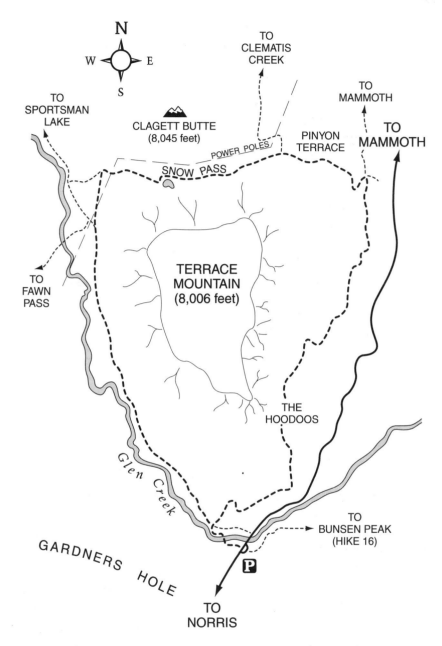

TERRACE MOUNTAIN
LOOP

Hike 19
Upper Falls, Lower Falls and Crystal Falls
Grand Canyon of the Yellowstone

Hiking distance: 3 miles round trip
Hiking time: 2 hours
Elevation gain: 600 feet
Maps: Trails Illustrated Mammoth Hot Springs, Tower/Canyon
The Yellowstone Association Canyon map
U.S.G.S. Canyon Village

Summary of hike: This hike takes you to three magnificent waterfalls in the Grand Canyon—Crystal Falls, with a 129-foot drop; Lower Falls, with a 308-foot drop (cover photo); and Upper Falls, with a 109-foot drop. A footbridge crosses over Cascade Creek just above Crystal Falls. For an awesome view of Lower Falls, follow the Brink of Falls Trail as it descends 600 feet into the canyon to the top of the falls.

Driving directions: From Canyon Junction, drive 1.6 miles south towards Fishing Bridge to the Upper Falls spur road on the left. Continue 0.2 miles and park in the parking lot.

Hiking directions: From the parking lot and restrooms, walk back along the side of the road about 200 yards to the North Rim Trail on the right. Take this trail a short distance to the canyon rim. From the rim is an excellent view of Crystal Falls. Continue on the trail towards the falls, and cross the footbridge over Cascade Creek. After crossing the bridge, several short trails to the right of the main trail lead to overlooks from the top of the falls. Continue along the main trail, which follows the rim of the canyon, to another footbridge on the left. Cross the bridge. The trail joins the Brink of Falls Trail and descends via switchbacks to the Lower Falls overlook at the very top of this magnificent falls. To return, take the same path back.

Back at the parking lot, take the trail to the southeast for a short quarter-mile round trip walk to the brink of Upper Falls, which plunges 109 feet. This side trip is well worth seeing.

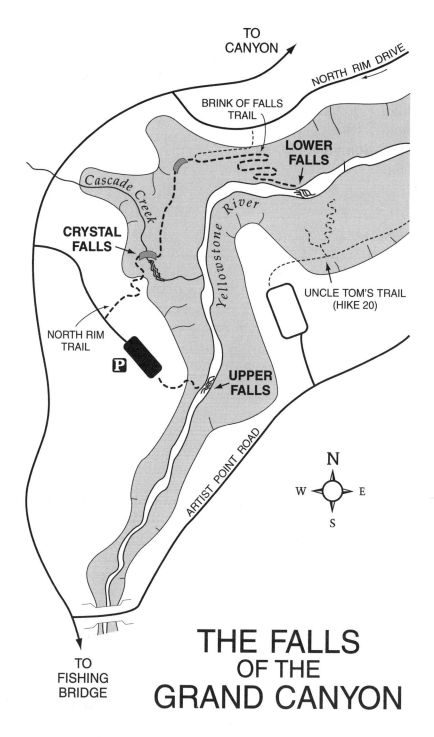

TO
CANYON

NORTH RIM DRIVE

BRINK OF FALLS
TRAIL

LOWER
FALLS

Cascade Creek

Yellowstone River

CRYSTAL
FALLS

UNCLE TOM'S TRAIL
(HIKE 20)

NORTH RIM
TRAIL

P

UPPER
FALLS

ARTIST POINT ROAD

N
W E
S

TO
FISHING
BRIDGE

THE FALLS
OF THE
GRAND CANYON

Hike 20
Uncle Tom's Trail
Grand Canyon of the Yellowstone

Hiking distance: 1 mile round trip
Hiking time: 1 hour
Elevation gain: 500 feet
Maps: Trails Illustrated Tower/Canyon
        The Yellowstone Association Canyon map
        U.S.G.S. Canyon Village

Summary of hike: This downhill hike along Uncle Tom's Trail utilizes a steep metal stairway into the 24-mile long Grand Canyon of the Yellowstone. These steps take you to an over-whelming view of the canyon at the base of the 308-foot Lower Falls. This trail offers close-up views of the rock spires and hoodoos in the eroded canyon walls. This hike is strenuous and not recommended for anyone without a healthy heart and lungs.

Driving directions: From Canyon Junction, drive 2.2 miles south towards Fishing Bridge. Turn left on Artist Point Road. Continue 0.6 miles to Uncle Tom's parking area on the left. Turn left and park. (The map for hike 21 is helpful for locating Uncle Tom's Trail.)

Hiking directions: From the far north end of the parking lot, take the trail north towards the canyon rim, then bear to the right. The trail descends via switchbacks to the stairs. Here begins the 328 metal stairs leading down into the canyon to the base of Lower Falls. Return to the trailhead the way you came.

The Brink of Falls Trail to the top of Lower Falls can be seen across the canyon (Hike 19).

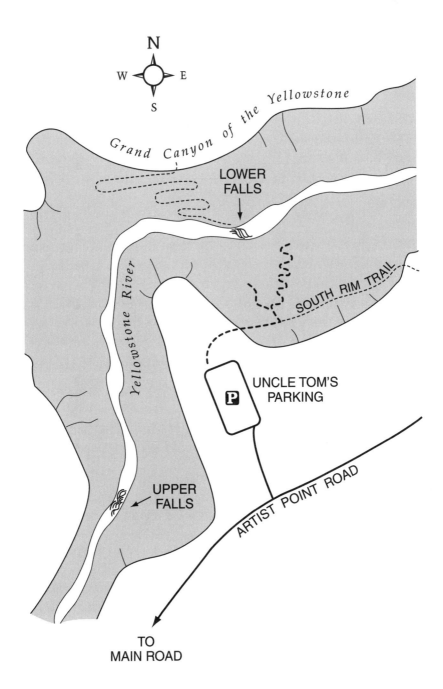

UNCLE TOM'S TRAIL

Hike 21
South Rim—Clear Lake Loop
Grand Canyon of the Yellowstone

Hiking distance: 3 miles round trip
Hiking time: 2 hours
Elevation gain: Near-level
Maps: Trails Illustrated Tower/Canyon
          The Yellowstone Association Canyon map
          U.S.G.S. Canyon Village

Summary of hike: This trail overlooks the Grand Canyon of
the Yellowstone and its two thundering waterfalls—Upper
and Lower Falls. The trail passes Lily Pad Lake en route to the
spring-fed Clear Lake, completely surrounded by forest in an
active thermal area containing boiling water holes and bubbling mud pots. It is a magnificent hike with a variety of
scenes.

Driving directions: From Canyon Junction, drive 2.2 miles
south towards Yellowstone Lake. Turn left on Artist Point
Road. Continue 0.6 miles to Uncle Tom's parking area on the
left. Turn left and park.

Hiking directions: From the parking area, walk north towards the canyon. The trail begins here and curves to the
right (east) along the rim to Artist Point. The trail reenters
civilization at the Artist Point parking lot and picks back up at
the end of the lot. From Artist Point, take the right junction to
Lily Pad Lake, which is a half mile ahead. After passing Lily Pad
Lake there is another trail junction. Take the right fork to Clear
Lake. (The left fork leads to Ribbon Lake, Hike 22.) Approxi-
mately 200 feet ahead is the beginning of the mud pots and
thermal pool area. This display of thermal activity continues
to Clear Lake. Shortly after passing Clear Lake is a trail junction. Take the right fork back to Uncle Tom's parking area.

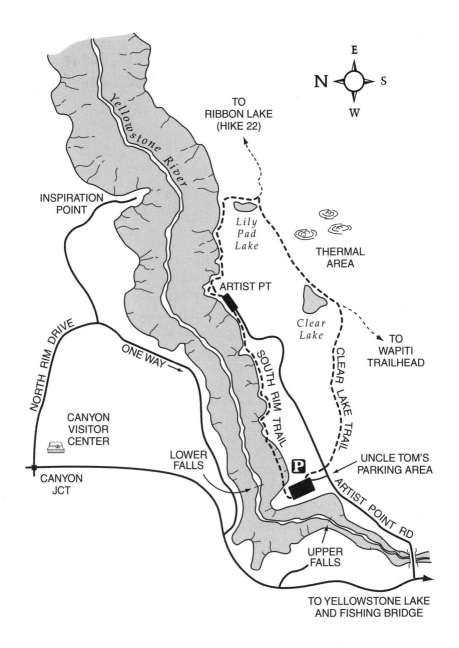

SOUTH RIM–CLEAR LAKE LOOP

Hike 22
Ribbon Lake and Silver Cord Cascade
Grand Canyon of the Yellowstone

Hiking distance: 4.2 miles round trip
Hiking time: 2 hours
Elevation gain: 300 feet
Maps: Trails Illustrated Tower/Canyon
      The Yellowstone Association Canyon map
      U.S.G.S. Canyon Village

Summary of hike: Ribbon Lake is actually two lakes that sit in a grassy meadow joined by a short, shallow stream. The hike to Ribbon Lake begins at Artist Point. The first part of the trail follows the edge of the Grand Canyon of the Yellowstone high above the Yellowstone River. Just beyond Ribbon Lake is an overlook by Silver Cord Cascade, a narrow 1,000-foot cascade dropping into the Grand Canyon.

Driving directions: From Canyon Junction, drive 2.2 miles south towards Yellowstone Lake. Turn left on Artist Point Road. Continue 1.5 miles to the Artist Point parking lot at the road's end. (The map for hike 21 is helpful for locating the parking lot.)

Hiking directions: Hike east on the paved path along the rim of the Grand Canyon of the Yellowstone. A short distance ahead is Artist Point—an overlook of the canyon and Lower Falls. Take the path to the right uphill towards Point Sublime. The trail follows the rim of the canyon for a half mile, then curves south and enters the forest. At 0.8 miles, cross a boardwalk over a marshy meadow to a trail fork at the south end of Lily Pad Lake. Take the left fork through the forest to a trail intersection by Ribbon Lake. Continue straight ahead. Bear left at another trail split, and head to the Silver Cord Cascade overlook at a rocky point on the canyon's rim. (The main trail loops around Ribbon Lake.) From the overlook, follow the canyon rim back towards Silver Cord Cascade. To return, reverse your route.

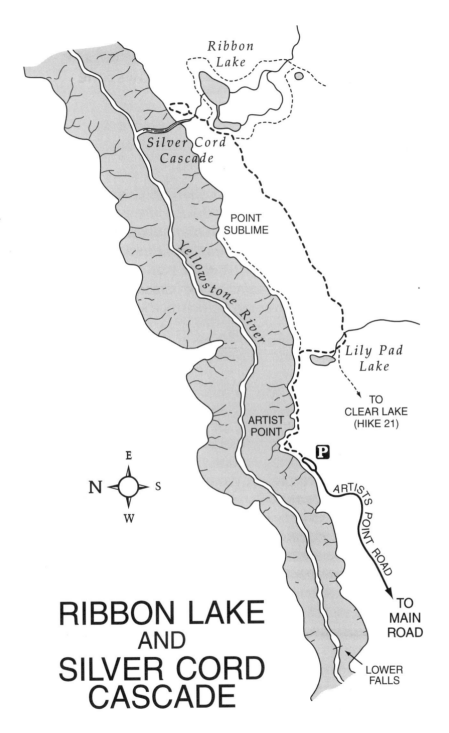

Ribbon Lake

Silver Cord Cascade

POINT
SUBLIME

Yellowstone River

Lily Pad Lake

TO
CLEAR LAKE
(HIKE 21)

ARTIST
POINT

P

ARTISTS POINT ROAD

TO
MAIN
ROAD

LOWER
FALLS

E

N   S

W

RIBBON LAKE
AND
SILVER CORD
CASCADE

Hike 23
Pahaska-Sunlight Trail to Sam Berry Meadow

Hiking distance: 7 miles round trip
Hiking time: 3.5 hours
Elevation gain: 250 feet
Maps: U.S.G.S. Pahaska Tepee

Summary of hike: The Pahaska-Sunlight Trail is an 18-mile trail beginning at the North Fork Shoshoni River near Pahaska Tepee just outside the east Yellowstone entrance. The trail heads north, eventually leading through Camp Monaco, a hunting camp established in 1913 by Buffalo Bill Cody during a trip with the Prince of Monaco. The trail ends in Sunlight Basin, the next major drainage to the north. This hike follows the first 3.5 miles of the trail along the North Fork Shoshoni River to Sam Berry Meadow. The grassy meadow sits on the banks of the river fringed with spruce and pines and has a primitive campsite. The trail has magnificent views of the surrounding peaks and the Sleeping Giant Winter Sports Area.

Driving directions: From the east entrance station of Yellowstone, drive east out of the park for 3.3 miles to the signed Pahaska-Sunlight Trailhead on the left. Turn left and drive 0.1 mile to the trailhead parking area.
From Cody, drive west on Highway 14-16-20 for 41.4 miles.

Hiking directions: Hike north past the trailhead sign and head uphill, entering a lodgepole pine and Douglas fir forest. Wind through the forest with panoramic views of the surrounding peaks. Cross small feeder streams. At 1.1 mile, the trail descends to the North Fork Shoshone River and a T-junction. Take the right fork upstream past a junction with the Crow Creek Trail on the left. Stay right, following the level watercourse through the burn area from the Clover Mist fire of 1988, which can be seen far up the meadow. At 3.5 miles, the trail reaches the Sam Berry Meadow. A side path leads down to the meadow and river. To return, retrace your steps.

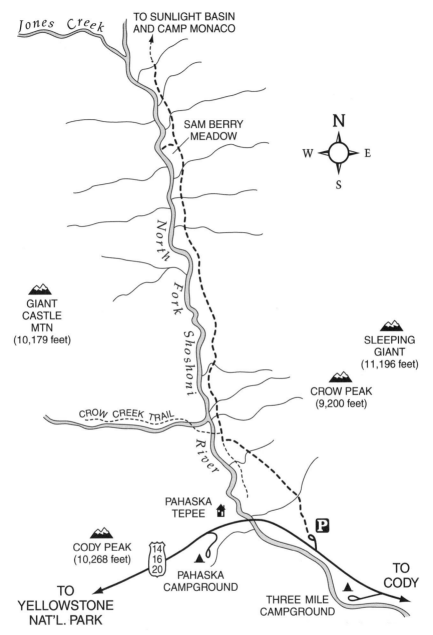

Jones Creek

TO SUNLIGHT BASIN
AND CAMP MONACO

SAM BERRY
MEADOW

N

W - E

S

North Fork Shoshoni River

GIANT
CASTLE
MTN
(10,179 feet)

SLEEPING
GIANT
(11,196 feet)

CROW PEAK
(9,200 feet)

CROW CREEK TRAIL

PAHASKA
TEPEE

P

CODY PEAK
(10,268 feet)

14
16
20

PAHASKA
CAMPGROUND

THREE MILE
CAMPGROUND

TO
CODY

TO
YELLOWSTONE
NAT'L. PARK

PAHASKA – SUNLIGHT
TRAIL

Hike 24
Storm Point Loop

Hiking distance: 2.5 mile loop
Hiking time: 1.5 hours
Elevation gain: Near-level
Maps: Trails Illustrated Yellowstone Lake
  U.S.G.S. Lake Butte

Summary of hike: This hike passes Indian Pond, a historic camping site for Indians, to the northeast shore of Yellowstone Lake. The trail leads through forests and meadows to Storm Point, a tree-covered rocky bluff overlooking the 87,000-acre Yellowstone Lake. In late spring and early summer, bears frequent this area.

Driving directions: From Fishing Bridge Visitor Center, drive 2.5 miles east towards the east park entrance. The turn-out and trailhead is on the right.

Hiking directions: From the parking turnout, the trail heads south through a meadow towards Yellowstone Lake. Within minutes is the north edge of Indian Pond, an ancient volcanic crater. The trail leads along the pond's west shore to Yellowstone Lake. From Yellowstone Lake, the trail follows the shoreline, heading south as it weaves in and out of the lodgepole forest. At one mile, the trail reaches the rocky Storm Point.

After exploring the rock peninsula of Storm Point, begin the return along the shoreline bluffs. In a few minutes, the trail will curve away from the shore through an old, dense lodgepole pine forest to the north. From this forest, emerge back into the meadow, cross a creek and head east towards Indian Pond to complete the loop.

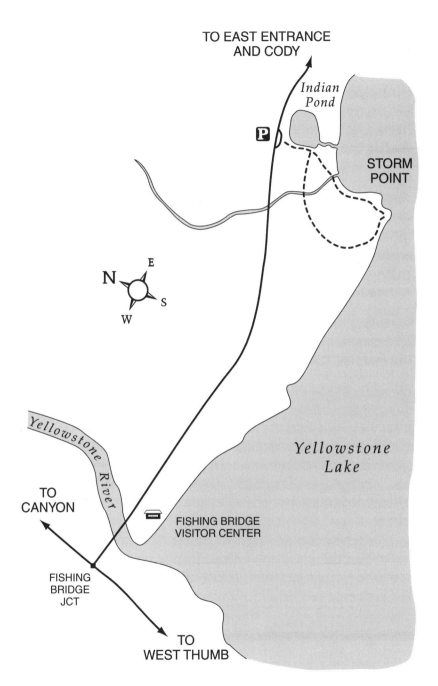

TO EAST ENTRANCE
AND CODY

Indian Pond

P

STORM POINT

N E S W

TO CANYON

Yellowstone River

Yellowstone Lake

FISHING BRIDGE VISITOR CENTER

FISHING BRIDGE JCT

TO WEST THUMB

STORM POINT LOOP

Hike 25
Pelican Creek Nature Trail

Hiking distance: 1 mile loop
Hiking time: 30 minutes
Elevation gain: Level
Maps: Trails Illustrated Yellowstone Lake
      U.S.G.S. Lake Butte

Summary of hike: The Pelican Creek Nature Trail follows Pelican Creek at its mouth where it meets Yellowstone Lake. The short, easy trail winds through the forest and across meadows to a beautiful sandy beach on the shores of Yellowstone Lake. From the beach are views of Stevenson Island and Mount Sheridan to the southwest.

Driving directions: From Fishing Bridge Junction, drive 1.5 miles east towards the east park entrance. The signed trailhead parking area is on the right.

Hiking directions: From the parking area, hike south through the lush lodgepole pine forest towards Yellowstone Lake. The loop begins thirty feet from the trailhead. Go to the right through the grove and meadows. At 0.4 miles is a trail fork. The right fork leads a few feet to Yellowstone Lake and a long sandy beach. The left fork continues east on the loop, paralleling the shore to another trail split. The left fork heads into the forest and fades out. Take the right fork down to the sandy beach. From the beach, the trail curves back into the forest, parallel to Pelican Creek. Cross a long wooden walkway across a grassy marsh, completing the loop near the trailhead.

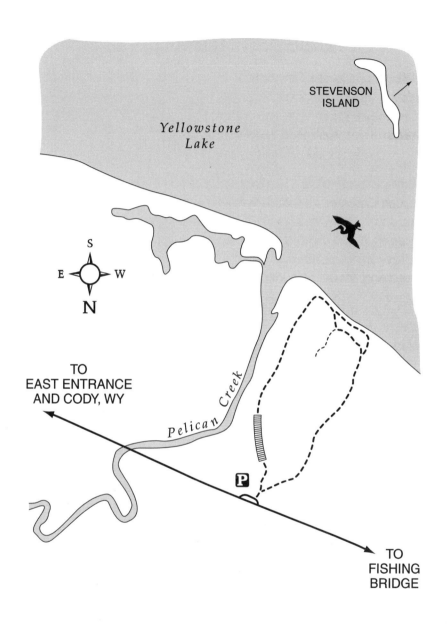

STEVENSON ISLAND

Yellowstone Lake

S

E ⊕ W

N

TO
EAST ENTRANCE
AND CODY, WY

Pelican Creek

P

TO
FISHING
BRIDGE

PELICAN CREEK
NATURE TRAIL

Hike 26
Elephant Back Loop

Hiking distance: 4 miles round trip
Hiking time: 2 hours
Elevation gain: 800 feet
Maps: Trails Illustrated Yellowstone Lake
U.S.G.S. Lake

Summary of hike: This trail through a dense forest climbs 800 feet up the elephant's back—a mountain shaped like an elephant from the aerial view. The highlight of this hike is a magnificent overlook of Yellowstone Lake and its beautiful green islands. From the overlook, Pelican Valley can be seen to the left while the Absaroka Mountain Range reaches skyward behind the lake.

Driving directions: From the Fishing Bridge Junction, drive 1.1 mile southwest towards West Thumb to the parking area on the right.

From the West Thumb Junction, drive 19.5 miles northeast towards Fishing Bridge to the parking area on the left.

Hiking directions: From the parking area, the trail parallels the road for a short distance, then curves to the right into the lodgepole forest and begins climbing. One mile from the trailhead is a trail junction, which is the beginning of the loop. The easier route is the trail to the left, circling in a clockwise direction. Switchbacks lead up to the summit and an overlook. From the Yellowstone Lake overlook, the trail loops back to the northeast. Descend along additional switchbacks and complete the loop. Return to the left, back to the parking area.

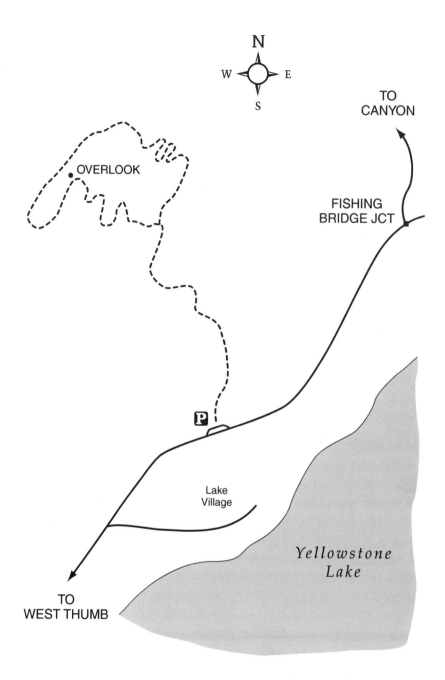

N
W E
S

TO
CANYON

OVERLOOK

FISHING
BRIDGE JCT

P

Lake
Village

*Yellowstone
Lake*

TO
WEST THUMB

ELEPHANT BACK LOOP

Hike 27
Natural Bridge Trail

Hiking distance: 3 miles round trip
Hiking time: 1.5 hours
Elevation gain: Near-level
Maps: Trails Illustrated Yellowstone Lake
        U.S.G.S. Lake

Summary of hike: The highlight of this trip is Natural Bridge, a 51-foot cliff with a 30-foot span over an opening cut through by frost and erosion. Once accessible by car, the forested road is now closed to vehicles and open to foot and bicycle traffic only.

Driving directions: From Fishing Bridge Junction, drive 3.1 miles southwest towards West Thumb. Turn right at the Bridge Bay Campground entrance. In a short distance, turn left and park in the Bridge Bay Marina parking lot.

Hiking directions: From the parking lot, hike north towards the campground to the trailhead. Follow the trail along the edge of the campground to a trail junction. Turn left into the forest as it winds around the west end of the marina. This forested trail meets a service road a half mile in from the trailhead. Go to the right and follow the paved service road one mile to Natural Bridge.

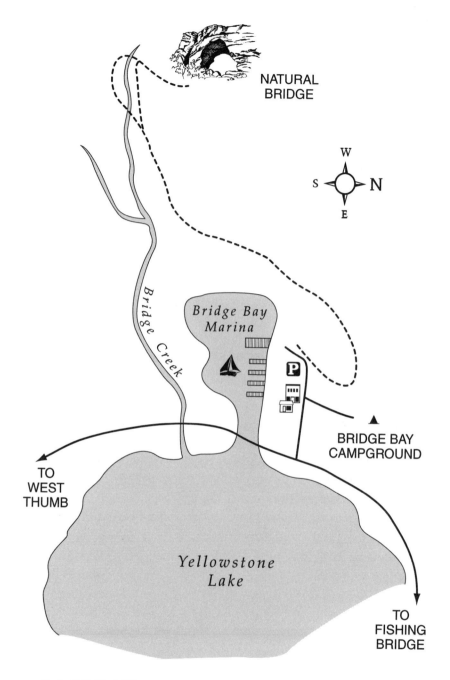

NATURAL BRIDGE

NATURAL BRIDGE TRAIL

Hike 28
Duck Lake

Hiking distance: 1 mile round trip
Hiking time: 30 minutes
Elevation gain: 200 feet
Maps: Trails Illustrated Yellowstone Lake
U.S.G.S. West Thumb

Summary of hike: Duck Lake is a 37-acre lake that sits in a deep basin at West Thumb, less than 0.2 miles from Yellowstone Lake. This half-mile trail follows a ridge between the two lakes with scenic views of the Absaroka Range across Yellowstone Lake. The trail begins adjacent to the West Thumb Geyser Basin, one of the smaller geyser basins in Yellowstone. A level half-mile boardwalk loops through the basin and along the shore of Yellowstone Lake.

Driving directions: At the West Thumb junction, park in the signed West Thumb Geyser Basin parking lot nearest the road.

Hiking directions: The signed trailhead is at the northwest corner of the parking lot near the road to Fishing Bridge. Take the path 20 yards and cross the road at the crosswalk. After crossing, head north up the gentle slope through the lodge-pole pine forest. Cross under power lines to a knoll over-looking Yellowstone Lake on the right and Duck Lake to the left. Follow the path on the east side of Duck Lake along the ridge separating the two bodies of water. Bear to the left and descend to the end of the trail at the lakeshore. Return along the same path.

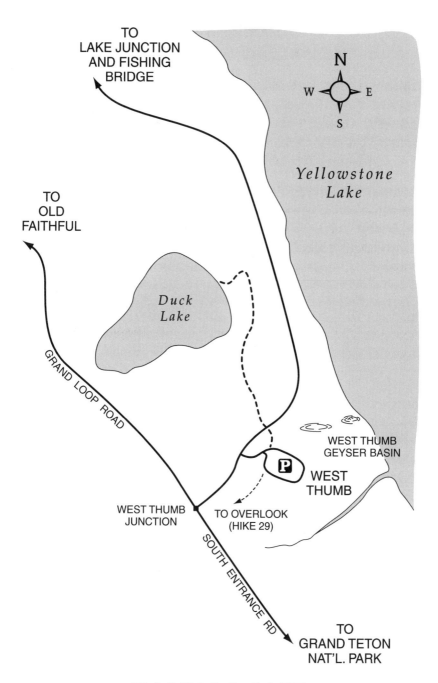

DUCK LAKE

Hike 29
Yellowstone Lake Overlook

Hiking distance: 2 mile loop
Hiking time: 1 hour
Elevation gain: 230 feet
Maps: Trails Illustrated Yellowstone Lake
   U.S.G.S. West Thumb

Summary of hike: The Yellowstone Lake Overlook is an easy hike to a knoll with commanding views of the West Thumb of Yellowstone Lake, Duck Lake (Hike 28), the West Thumb Geyser Basin and the Absaroka Range. The trail heads through a forest and high mountain meadow to the overlook. The Continental Divide lies just a few miles to the southwest.

Driving directions: At the West Thumb junction, park in the signed West Thumb Geyser Basin parking lot nearest the road.

Hiking directions: Head southwest past the trail sign. Walk across the grassy meadow with stands of pines. Cross the South Entrance Road, and continue through the forest to a log bridge and "Overlook" sign. Begin the loop portion of the hike by crossing the bridge to the right. Wind through the partially burned forest past dormant thermal depressions. Climb up a small rise, then cross the level ridge to the second hill. Ascend the second hill to a side path on the right. Head up the side path to the overlook with an old log bench and down trees to sit on. After enjoying the views, return to the main trail and continue to the right. Head through an open forest, then through a burned forest. Return to the log bridge, completing the loop. Cross the road and return to the trailhead.

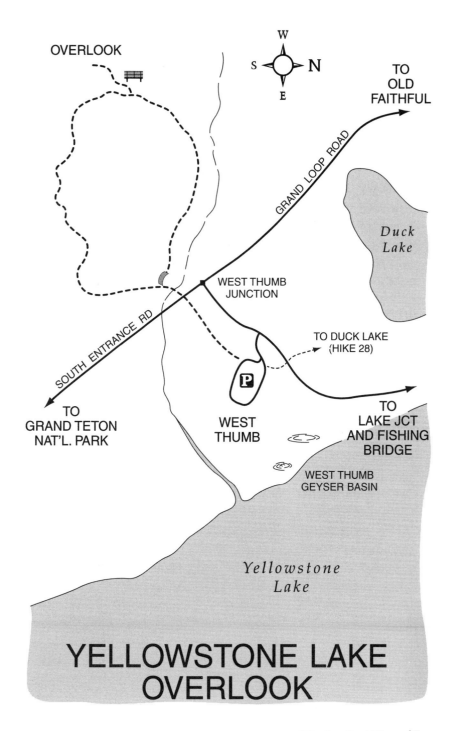

OVERLOOK

W
N
S
E

TO
OLD
FAITHFUL

GRAND LOOP ROAD

Duck Lake

WEST THUMB
JUNCTION

SOUTH ENTRANCE RD

TO DUCK LAKE
(HIKE 28)

P

TO
GRAND TETON
NAT'L. PARK

WEST
THUMB

TO
LAKE JCT
AND FISHING
BRIDGE

WEST THUMB
GEYSER BASIN

Yellowstone Lake

YELLOWSTONE LAKE OVERLOOK

Hike 30
Riddle Lake Trail

Hiking distance: 5 miles round trip
Hiking time: 2.5 hours
Elevation gain: Level
Maps: Trails Illustrated Old Faithful
U.S.G.S. Mount Sheridan

Summary of hike: The Riddle Lake Trail is an easy hike through a lodgepole forest and meadows patterned with streams. Although the hike is level, Riddle Lake is located only one mile from the Continental Divide. The 274-acre lake and the marsh to its west are home to a large variety of birds. The trail heads to the north of the lake and bypasses the marsh. However, the area can be wet in May and June. Mosquito repellent is recommended.

Driving directions: From the West Thumb Junction, drive 4 miles south towards Grand Teton National Park to the trailhead parking area on the left. It is located 0.1 mile past the large Continental Divide sign.

Hiking directions: From the parking area, the trail is easy to see and leads east through the forest away from the highway. The clearly defined trail crosses the Continental Divide, yet there is little change in elevation. Continue through the forest to the north shore of the lake and a small beach. To return, retrace your steps.

Additional note: This area is a bear management area. The Park Service has been closing the area to humans from April 30 through mid-July. Closing the area allows the bears to pursue their natural behavior patterns without disturbance.

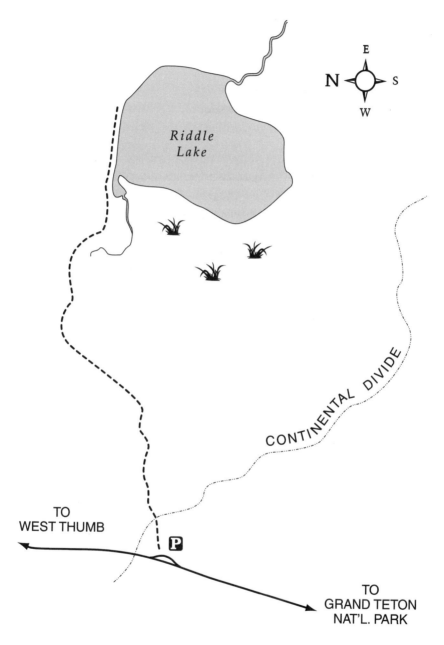

Riddle
Lake

E
N
W
S

CONTINENTAL DIVIDE

TO
WEST THUMB

P

TO
GRAND TETON
NAT'L. PARK

RIDDLE LAKE

Hike 31
Lone Star Geyser Trail

Hiking distance: 5 miles round trip
Hiking time: 2 hours
Elevation gain: 200 feet
Maps: Trails Illustrated Old Faithful
U.S.G.S. Old Faithful

Summary of hike: This beautiful, near-level hike parallels the Firehole River all the way to Lone Star Geyser. There are few people here, and the area is undeveloped, making this more of a wilderness experience. The isolated 12-foot sinter cone geyser is one of the largest cones in Yellowstone. Lone Star Geyser erupts in three-hour intervals, shooting 30 to 50 feet high. The memorable eruption is well worth waiting for.

Driving directions: The Lone Star Geyser Trail is south of Old Faithful on the road between Madison Junction and West Thumb. From Old Faithful, take the road south towards West Thumb 3.7 miles to the Lone Star Geyser parking area. It is located about 50 yards past the well-marked Kepler Cascades. Turn right and park.

Hiking directions: Hike south on the level trail, an old road, through the beautiful forest. The trail parallels the east banks of the Firehole River. Cross the bridge over the river, and continue upstream on the west side of the river. At two miles is a junction with Spring Creek Trail. Stay to the right, heading south to the Lone Star Geyser at 2.5 miles. After experiencing the eruption, return by taking the same trail back.

Back at the parking lot, take a side trip 50 yards to Kepler Cascades, where the Firehole River dramatically drops 125 feet in a narrow canyon.

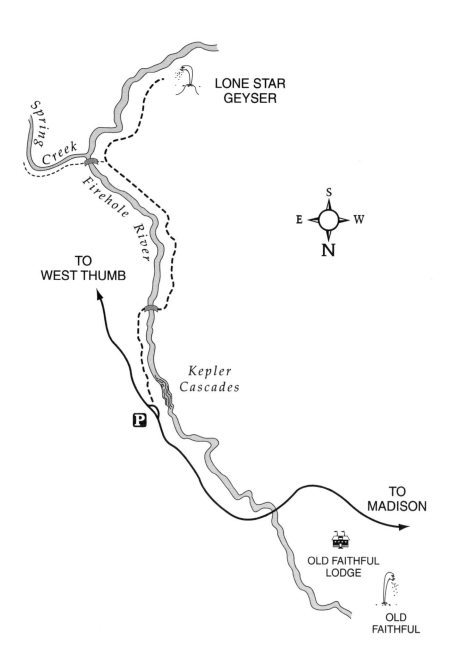

LONE STAR GEYSER

Hike 32
Upper Geyser Basin
The Boardwalks at Old Faithful

Hiking distance: 2 to 4 miles round trip
Hiking time: 1 to 3 hours
Elevation gain: Level
Maps: Trails Illustrated Old Faithful
       The Yellowstone Association Upper Geyser map
       U.S.G.S. Old Faithful

Summary of hike: Although this is not a backcountry hike, except for the Observation Point trail, it is magnificent and a favorite Yellowstone hike. The Upper Geyser Basin (photo on back cover) contains the largest group of geysers in the world, including Old Faithful. They are in continuous motion. The predicted times of many of their eruptions are posted in the visitor center. Viewing this large assortment of geysers, pools, and the Firehole River make this walk a chance to see one of the earth's magical wonders.

Driving directions: Old Faithful is located between Madison and West Thumb Junctions. Exit from the main road into the Old Faithful parking complex. This hike begins near the Old Faithful visitor center.

Hiking directions: From the parking lot or visitor center, walk towards Old Faithful Geyser. The boardwalks and improved trails will lead you along various loops. Whichever direction you decide to take, you will feel you chose the right route.

To arrive at Observation Point, cross the first Firehole River bridge, and take the 1.3-mile Geyser Hill loop. From Observation Point, there is a beautiful overview of the Upper Geyser Basin and the magnificent thermal activity.

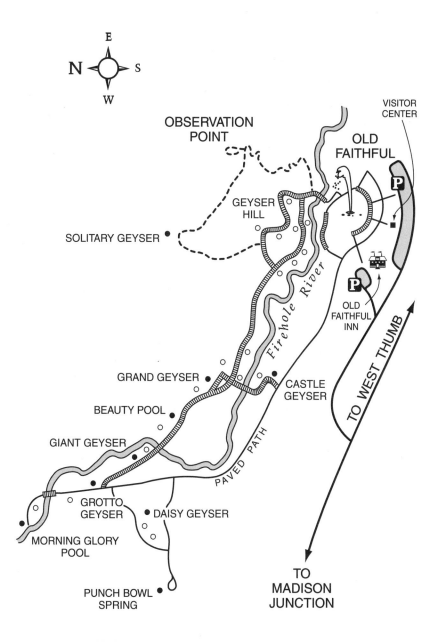

UPPER GEYSER BASIN
BOARDWALKS

Hike 33
Mystic Falls Loop

Hiking distance: 3 miles round trip
Hiking time: 1.5 hours
Elevation gain: 800 feet
Maps: Trails Illustrated Old Faithful
U.S.G.S. Old Faithful

Summary of hike: This hike follows the Little Firehole River to Mystic Falls—a full-bodied, powerful waterfall cascading down several benches with a total drop of 100 feet. The backcountry portion of the trail also includes an overlook of Biscuit Basin. The wooden walkways at the beginning of the hike meander through the thermal pools and geysers of this basin. Many people visit this area specifically to view these thermal features.

Driving directions: Mystic Falls is on the road between Old Faithful and Madison Junction. From Old Faithful, drive north 2.5 miles to the Biscuit Basin parking area. Turn left and park. From Madison Junction, drive south 13.8 miles to the Biscuit Basin parking area and turn right.

Hiking directions: From the parking lot, cross the bridge over the Firehole River. Walk to the far end of the wooden boardwalk, past the pools and geysers, where you will find the signed trail that leads to Mystic Falls. At the first junction, take the lower trail to the left. This is the beginning of the loop. The lower trail parallels the Little Firehole River to Mystic Falls. Near the falls, continue on the trail as you climb up switchbacks to the top of the falls. The trail continues up to a ridge. Follow the ridge along the edge of the Madison Plateau to an overlook of the surrounding geyser basins. Switchbacks lead back down to the boardwalk at Biscuit Basin, returning to the trailhead.

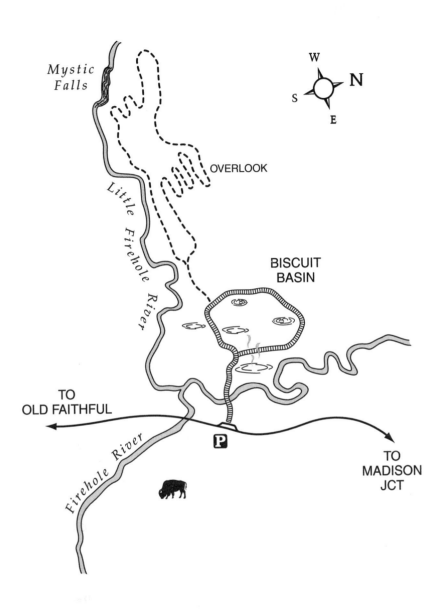

Mystic Falls

Little Firehole River

OVERLOOK

BISCUIT BASIN

TO OLD FAITHFUL

Firehole River

P

TO MADISON JCT

W N S E

MYSTIC FALLS LOOP

Hike 34
Fairy Falls

Hiking distance: 5.2 miles round trip
Hiking time: 2.5 hours
Elevation gain: Near level
Maps: Trails Illustrated Old Faithful
U.S.G.S. Lower Geyser Basin

Summary of hike: Fairy Falls is a slender, 200-foot vertical waterfall that splashes into a beautiful pool in a shady rock grotto. This near-level hike skirts the edge of Midway Geyser Basin past geysers and springs parallel to the Firehole River. The path leads through a lodgepole pine forest that was burned to a crisp in the 1988 fire. It is fascinating to see the growth of the new trees carpeting the valley floor.

Driving directions: The Fairy Falls Trailhead is located between Old Faithful and Madison Junction. From Old Faithful, drive 4.6 miles north to the signed Fairy Falls turnoff on the left. Turn left and park 0.1 mile ahead in the parking lot. From Madison Junction, drive 11.5 miles south to the signed Fairy Falls turnoff on the right.

Hiking directions: Cross the steel bridge over the Firehole River, and head northwest along the wide Fountain Flat Drive trail. The path parallels the Firehole River along the southwest side of the Midway Geyser Basin, passing Grand Prismatic Spring and Excelsior Geyser Crater. At one mile is a signed junction with the Fairy Falls Trail. Bear left and continue west on the footpath. Walk across the gentle terrain and through the burned area, arriving at the base of Fairy Falls. After enjoying the falls and pool, return to the trailhead along the same trail.

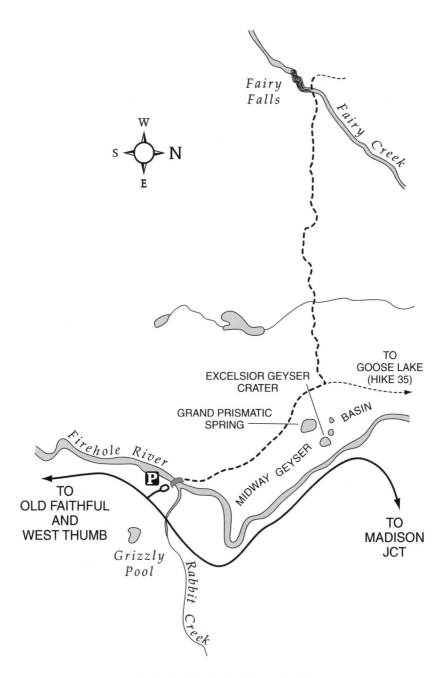

FAIRY FALLS

Hike 35
Goose Lake and Feather Lake

Hiking distance: 5.2 miles round trip
Hiking time: 2.5 hours
Elevation gain: Near level
Maps: Trails Illustrated Old Faithful
　　　　 U.S.G.S. Lower Geyser Basin

Summary of hike: Goose Lake and Feather Lake sit in a natural depression formed by volcanic and thermal activity. Both lakes lie alongside the Firehole River and are surrounded by lodgepole pines. This hike leads through a beautiful meadow with hot springs and thermal mounds to the lakes. The lakes are accessible and easy to hike around. Goose Lake has rainbow trout but Feather Lake is fishless.

Driving directions: The trailhead is located between Old Faithful and Madison Junction. From Old Faithful, drive 10.5 miles north to Fountain Flat Drive on the left. Turn left and drive 0.8 miles to the trailhead parking lot at the end of the road. From Madison Junction, drive 5.6 miles south to Fountain Flat Drive on the right.

Hiking directions: Head south on Fountain Flat Drive, a graveled road which is closed to vehicles. Follow the road past Ojo Caliente Spring, a hot spring on the right, and cross the bridge over the Firehole River at 0.4 miles. Continue along the wide level trail, reaching the northwest corner of Goose Lake at 1.7 miles. Stay on Fountain Flat Drive along the southwest side of Goose Lake to a junction at 2.2 miles. The trail straight ahead to the south leads 2.2 miles to Fairy Falls (Hike 34). Bear left and follow the Firehole River less than a half mile downstream through the grassy meadow to a picnic area at Feather Lake. Hiking around either lake is easy. At the north end of the lakes is a circular three-acre pond. Complete your own loop back to Fountain Flat Drive. Go to the right, heading back along the same route.

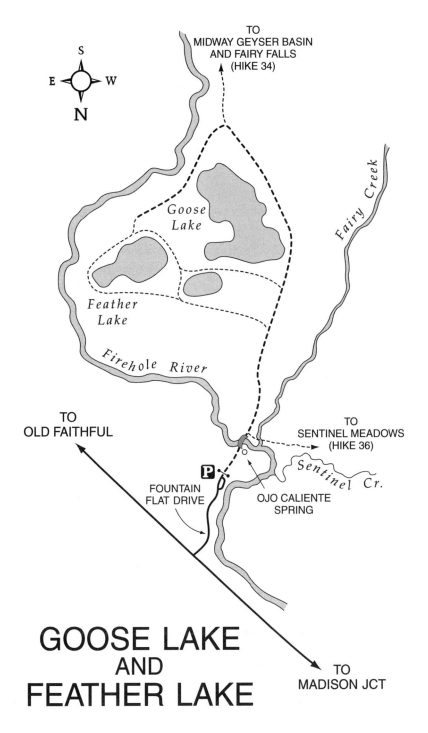

TO
MIDWAY GEYSER BASIN
AND FAIRY FALLS
(HIKE 34)

S

E — W

N

Goose Lake

Fairy Creek

Feather Lake

Firehole River

TO
OLD FAITHFUL

TO
SENTINEL MEADOWS
(HIKE 36)

Sentinel Cr.

P

FOUNTAIN
FLAT DRIVE

OJO CALIENTE
SPRING

GOOSE LAKE
AND
FEATHER LAKE

TO
MADISON JCT

Hike 36
Sentinel Meadows

Hiking distance: 3.8 miles round trip
Hiking time: 2 hours
Elevation gain: Near level
Maps: Trails Illustrated Old Faithful
U.S.G.S. Lower Geyser Basin

Summary of hike: The hike through Sentinel Meadows leads to Queens Laundry, a small thermal area also known as Red Terrace Spring. In the 1880s, the spring at the west end of the meadow was used as a bathing area. A log bath house was built and the structure still remains. Sentinel Creek weaves through the meadow. This hike follows the flat open meadow, passing numerous hot spring mounds.

Driving directions: Follow the driving directions for Hike 35 to the trailhead parking lot on Fountain Flat Drive.

Hiking directions: Head south on Fountain Flat Drive, which is closed to vehicles. Follow the road past Ojo Caliente Spring, a hot spring on the right along the Firehole River. Cross the bridge over the river to a signed trail on the right at 0.4 miles. Bear right, heading downstream through the meadow. Cross a footbridge over Fairy Creek. Continue through a burned forest from the 1988 fires, then descend into an open meadow with stands of lodgepole pines. Cross a log bridge over a meandering stream. The trail becomes faint near an orange trail junction sign on a tree. Straight ahead through the meadow are hot thermal mounds. This route can be wet and marshy in spots. If so, take the left route towards campsite OG2, leading up a knoll. This trail follows the south edge of Sentinel Meadows along the hillside. At the west end of the meadow is Queens Laundry. After exploring the area, return along the same trail. The trail also loops back to Fountain Flat Drive on the Imperial Meadows Trail, but the trail is difficult to follow and not recommended.

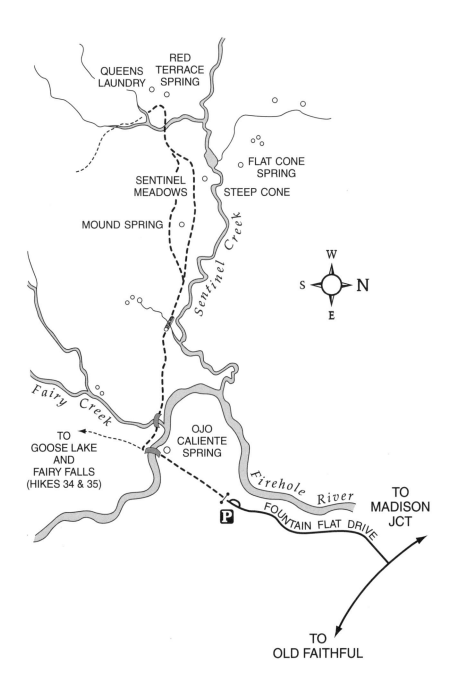

QUEENS LAUNDRY

RED TERRACE SPRING

FLAT CONE SPRING

SENTINEL MEADOWS

STEEP CONE

MOUND SPRING

Sentinel Creek

W
S · N
E

Fairy Creek

TO GOOSE LAKE AND FAIRY FALLS (HIKES 34 & 35)

OJO CALIENTE SPRING

Firehole River

P

FOUNTAIN FLAT DRIVE

TO MADISON JCT

TO OLD FAITHFUL

SENTINEL MEADOW

Hike 37
Nez Perce Creek

Hiking distance: 4 miles round trip
Hiking time: 2 hours
Elevation gain: Near level
Maps: Trails Illustrated Old Faithful
　　　　U.S.G.S. Lower Geyser Basin

Summary of hike: This hike parallels Nez Perce Creek through Culex Basin, a beautiful valley fringed with pine forests. The basin is home to the Morning Mist Springs, a group of hot springs, thermal pools, sinter mounds and some geysers. The hike follows the Mary Mountain Trail, an old road closed in the 1970s. The trail passes numerous hot springs and thermal areas to a bridge crossing Nez Perce Creek.

Driving directions: From Old Faithful, drive 9.9 miles north to the paved parking pullouts on either side of the road south of Nez Perce Creek. From Madison Junction, drive 6.2 miles south to the paved parking pullouts after crossing Nez Perce Creek.

Hiking directions: Head east on the footpath along the south edge of Nez Perce Creek past the forested, pyramid-shaped Porcupine Hills. Along the winding creek are thermal areas and hot springs. In a half mile on the right is Morning Mist Springs, a group of thermal springs and hot clear pools. As the trail fades away, cross the meadow while exploring the various pools, then join the Mary Mountain Trail. (The Mary Mountain Trail begins at the park road in the signed parking area 0.3 miles south of Nez Perce Creek.) Bear left, heading up the valley. The trail parallels the creek past a continuous series of boiling pots, hot springs and clear pools. At two miles the road ends at a wooden footbridge crossing Nez Perce Creek. This is our turnaround spot.

To hike further, the trail follows the creek up to Mary Lake near the summit of Mary Mountain, nine miles further.

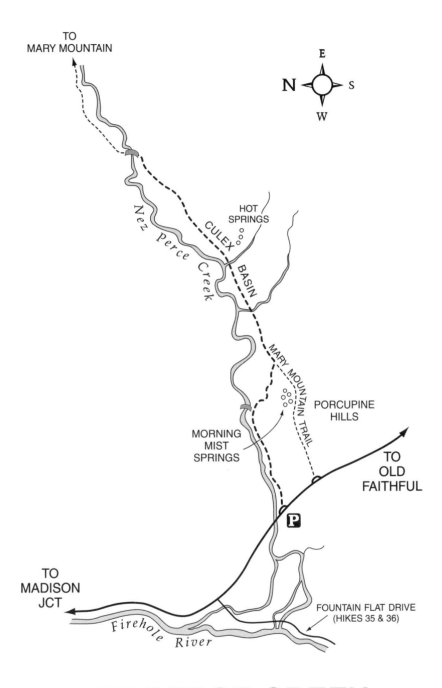

NEZ PERCE CREEK

Hike 38
Monument Geyser Basin Trail

Hiking distance: 3 miles round trip
Hiking time: 1.5 hours
Elevation gain: 650 feet
Maps: Trails Illustrated Mammoth Hot Springs
       U.S.G.S. Norris Junction and Madison Junction

Summary of hike: The first part of this hike follows beside the Gibbon River on the south edge of Gibbon Meadows. The trail then climbs a hill to a thermal area with unusual sinter cones, mud pots, steam vents and sulfur caldrons. A special feature of this hike is that few people hike the trail, so you may receive a private showing.

The fires of 1988 burned the lodgepole trees in this area. A new covering of healthy lodgepoles now blanket the ground.

Driving directions: The Monument Geyser Basin turnout is located 8.6 miles northeast from Madison Junction and 4.7 miles southwest from Norris Junction. The turnout is on the west side of the road just south of the bridge crossing the Gibbon River. A small Park Service sign reads "Monument" at the turnout.

Hiking directions: From the parking turnout, walk upstream along the west side of the Gibbon River. After a half mile, the trail curves west away from the river and climbs steadily uphill through the forest, gaining 650 feet. At the top of the hill, veer to the right a short distance to this unique area. After exploring the formations, return along the same trail.

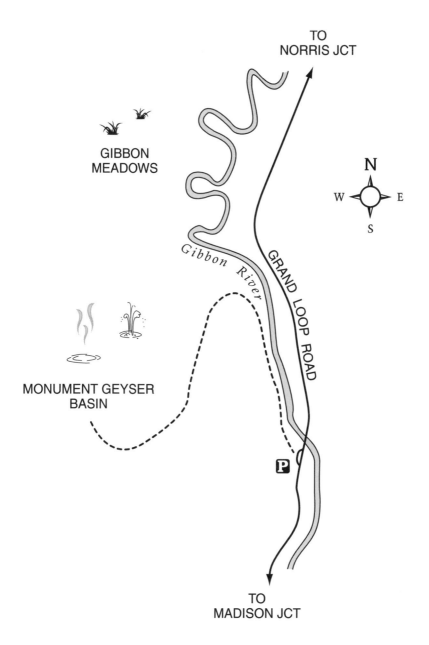

TO
NORRIS JCT

GIBBON
MEADOWS

Gibbon River

GRAND LOOP ROAD

N
W   E
S

MONUMENT GEYSER
BASIN

P

TO
MADISON JCT

MONUMENT GEYSER
BASIN TRAIL

Hike 39
Artists Paintpots Trail

Hiking distance: 1.2 miles round trip
Hiking time: 40 minutes
Elevation gain: 100 feet
Maps: Trails Illustrated Mammoth Hot Springs
      U.S.G.S. Norris Junction

Summary of hike: The Artists Paintpots Trail tours a variety of hot pots and pools of various colors (blue, red, brown and green), steam vents and a hypnotizing boiling mud pot. The paintpots are located on the south edge of Gibbon Meadows. The trail does not get heavy foot traffic, which allows an opportunity to savor these thermal treats privately. Part of the trail follows a boardwalk.

Driving directions: The Artists Paintpots parking area is located 9.3 miles northeast from Madison Junction and 4 miles southwest from Norris Junction. The turnout is on the east side of the road at the south edge of Gibbon Meadows.

Hiking directions: From the parking turnout, follow the walkway east along the base of a burned hillside of the 1988 fires. This trail leads through the flat thermal area to a junction, beginning the loop. Stay to the left in the basin, then climb up Paintpot Hill to the south. From the top is a vista of the colorful thermal area below. The trail loops back along the hilltop overlooking the area. From the large boiling mud pot, the trail descends to the right and back to the bottom, completing the loop. Return along the trail to the parking turnout.

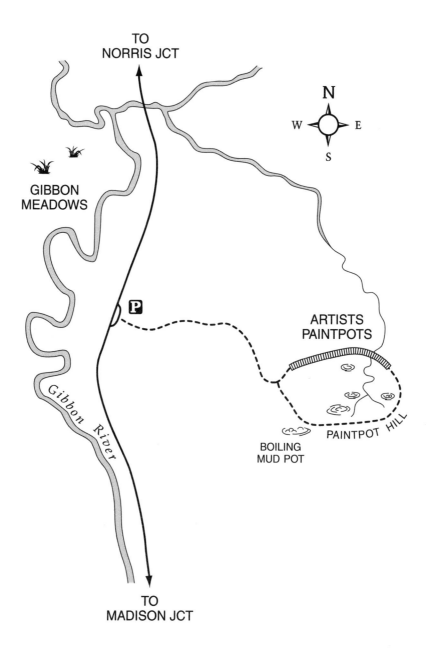

TO
NORRIS JCT

N
W E
S

GIBBON
MEADOWS

P

ARTISTS
PAINTPOTS

Gibbon River

PAINTPOT HILL

BOILING
MUD POT

TO
MADISON JCT

ARTISTS PAINTPOTS
TRAIL

Hike 40
Harlequin Lake Trail

Hiking distance: 1 mile round trip
Hiking time: 30 minutes
Elevation gain: 120 feet
Maps: Trails Illustrated Old Faithful
U.S.G.S. Mount Jackson

Summary of hike: The Harlequin Lake Trail is a short, easy hike to a 10-acre secluded lake. The circular lake is half covered in lily pads with bright yellow flowers. A variety of birds inhabit the area, but the lake does not have fish. The Yellowstone fires of 1988 burned the lodgepole trees surrounding this trail, and thousands of new lodgepole pines now cover the hillside.

Driving directions: Harlequin Lake is on the road between West Yellowstone and Madison Junction. From the West Yellowstone Park entrance, drive east 11.9 miles and turn right into the parking area on the south side of the road. From Madison Junction, drive west 1.6 miles and turn left into the parking area. On the north side of the highway is a sign marked "Harlequin Lake."

Hiking directions: Cross the highway to the signed Harlequin Lake trailhead. The trail gently climbs around the hill, curving to the left. Tucked in on the other side of the hill is Harlequin Lake. The trail follows the south side of the lake and fades out. At the north end of the lake is a steep hillside. To return, take the same trail back.

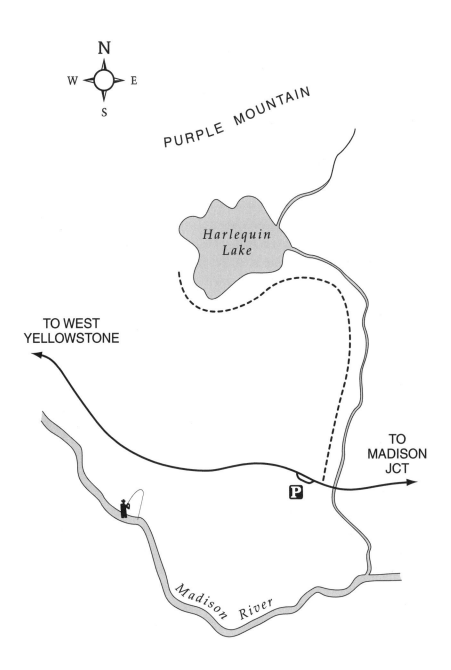

N
W   E
S

PURPLE MOUNTAIN

Harlequin Lake

TO WEST
YELLOWSTONE

TO
MADISON
JCT

P

Madison River

HARLEQUIN LAKE

Hike 41
Gneiss Creek Trail
from the Madison River

Hiking distance: 2.8 miles round trip
Hiking time: 1.5 hours
Elevation gain: 150 feet
Maps: Trails Illustrated Mammoth Hot Springs
U.S.G.S. Mount Jackson

Summary of hike: The Gneiss Creek Trail is a 14-mile trail through the Madison Valley connecting the Madison Canyon with the Gallatin to the north. This hike follows the first portion of the trail from the southern trailhead at the Madison River. The trail eventually connects to the northern trailhead, Hike 50.

Driving directions: The Gneiss Creek Trail is on the road between West Yellowstone and Madison Junction. From the West Yellowstone Park entrance, drive 7.3 miles east to the signed Gneiss Trail on the left, just after crossing the Madison River Bridge. From Madison Junction, drive 6.2 miles west to the trailhead parking lot on the right, just before crossing the Madison River Bridge.

Hiking directions: Walk northwest along the north shore of the Madison River, heading downstream. The path hugs the edge of the steep forested cliffs along the riverbank. There are frequent rises, dips and deadfall trees. At 0.8 miles, the trail curves right, away from the Madison River, and climbs a hill to a ridge. Head north through the burned Douglas fir and lodgepole pine forest. At 1.4 miles is a signed junction with the Cougar Creek Trail. This is our turnaround spot.

To hike further, the Cougar Creek Trail bears right, heading northeast to a patrol cabin on the creek. The Gneiss Creek Trail continues to the left, skirting the east edge of the Madison Valley to the northern trailhead 12.5 miles ahead.

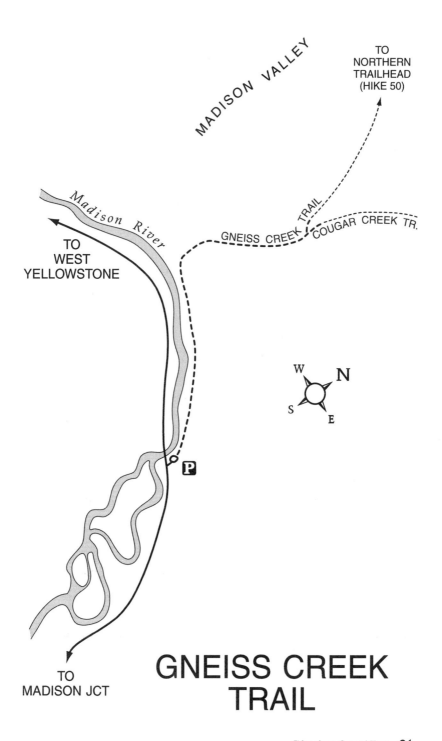

MADISON VALLEY

TO
NORTHERN
TRAILHEAD
(HIKE 50)

Madison River

GNEISS CREEK TRAIL

COUGAR CREEK TR.

TO
WEST
YELLOWSTONE

W N
S E

P

GNEISS CREEK TRAIL

TO
MADISON JCT

Hike 42
Tepee Creek Trail to Tepee Pass

Hiking distance: 6 miles round trip
Hiking time: 3 hours
Elevation gain: 900 feet
Maps: U.S.G.S. Sunshine Point

Summary of hike: The Tepee Creek Trail follows up the watercourse of Tepee Creek through expansive grasslands to Tepee Pass at the head of the verdant valley. From Tepee Pass are tremendous sweeping views down the wide valley and beyond, from the Madison Range to the Gallatin Range.

Driving directions: From West Yellowstone, drive 33 miles north on Highway 191 (towards Bozeman) to the signed trail on the right by mile marker 32. Turn right and park 100 yards ahead by the trailhead.

From Big Sky, take Highway 191 south for 16 miles to the trailhead on the left.

Hiking directions: Head northeast up the wide grassy draw between Sunshine Point and Crown Butte. Follow the trail along Tepee Creek to a signed junction at 1.1 mile. The right fork crosses Tepee Creek and leads eastward to the park boundary (Hike 43). Take the left fork towards Tepee Pass and Buffalo Horn Divide. Climb a small hill, then traverse the hillside above the valley. Continue past the prominent Grouse Mountain and stands of aspens and pines. After numerous dips and rises along the rolling ridges, the trail begins a half-mile ascent to Tepee Pass. At the top of the valley near a dense stand of evergreens, there is a signed four-way junction on Tepee Pass. The right fork leads 200 yards to a flat area above the saddle with great views. This is our turnaround spot.

To hike further, the east trail leads two miles to the Yellowstone National Park boundary. From Tepee Pass, a trail descends to the north for 2.5 miles to Buffalo Horn Creek. To the west, a trail leads down Wilson Draw to the Gallatin River.

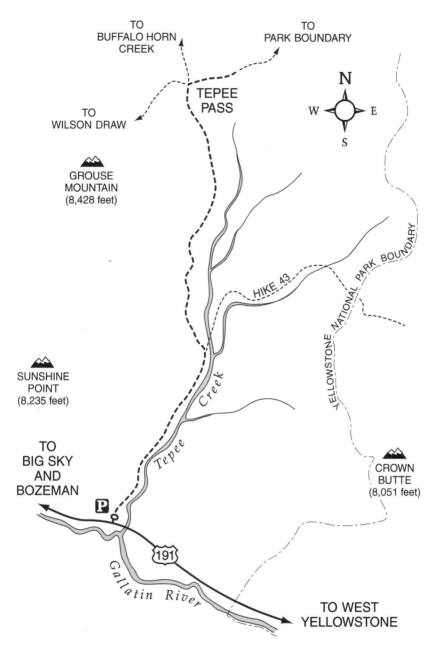

TO
BUFFALO HORN
CREEK

TO
PARK BOUNDARY

TEPEE
PASS

N
W E
S

TO
WILSON DRAW

GROUSE
MOUNTAIN
(8,428 feet)

HIKE 43

YELLOWSTONE NATIONAL PARK BOUNDARY

SUNSHINE
POINT
(8,235 feet)

Tepee Creek

TO
BIG SKY
AND
BOZEMAN

CROWN
BUTTE
(8,051 feet)

P

191

Gallatin River

TO WEST
YELLOWSTONE

TEPEE CREEK TRAIL
TO TEPEE PASS

Hike 43
Tepee Creek Trail to the
Yellowstone National Park Boundary

Hiking distance: 4.6 miles round trip
Hiking time: 2.5 hours
Elevation gain: 700 feet
Maps: U.S.G.S. Sunshine Point

Summary of hike: The Tepee Creek Trail begins just outside the northwest corner of Yellowstone National Park. The trail crosses gentle slopes through a broad grassy valley, passing dense tree-lined ridges. The hike ends on a grassy ridgetop at the Yellowstone boundary overlooking the Daly Creek drainage.

Driving directions: From West Yellowstone, drive 33 miles north on Highway 191 (towards Bozeman) to the signed trail on the right by mile marker 32. Turn right and park 100 yards ahead by the trailhead.

From Big Sky, take Highway 191 south for 16 miles to the trailhead on the left.

Hiking directions: Hike northeast past the hitching posts, and cross the grassy slopes along the base of Sunshine Point. Follow the open expanse along the west side of Tepee Creek to a signed junction at 1.1 mile. The left fork heads north to Tepee Pass and Buffalo Horn Creek (Hike 42). Take the right fork across Tepee Creek, and continue up the hillside on the east side of the creek. The trail curves to the right and heads east up a narrow drainage surrounded by mountains and tree groves. Near the top of a meadow, follow the ridge to the signed Yellowstone boundary on the saddle. Just below the saddle is a pond. Return to the trailhead the way you came.

To hike further, the trail descends into Yellowstone to Daly Creek (Hike 44).

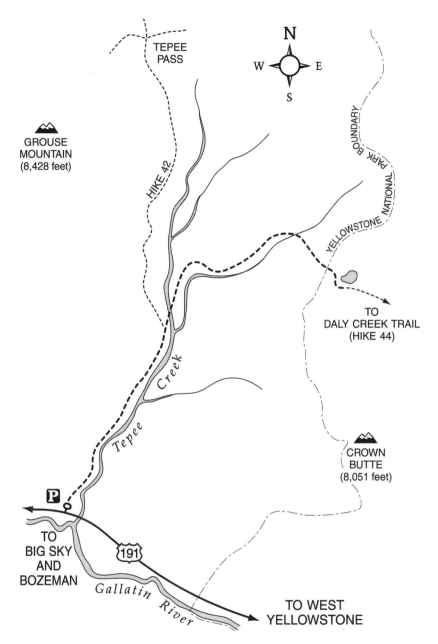

TEPEE PASS

N
W • E
S

GROUSE
MOUNTAIN
(8,428 feet)

HIKE 42

YELLOWSTONE NATIONAL PARK BOUNDARY

TO
DALY CREEK TRAIL
(HIKE 44)

Tepee Creek

CROWN
BUTTE
(8,051 feet)

P

TO
BIG SKY
AND
BOZEMAN

191

Gallatin River

TO WEST
YELLOWSTONE

TEPEE CREEK TRAIL
TO PARK BOUNDARY

Hike 44
Daly Creek Trail

Hiking distance: 5.2 miles round trip
Hiking time: 2.5 hours
Elevation gain: 350 feet
Maps: Trails Illustrated Mammoth Hot Springs
U.S.G.S. Sunshine Point and Big Horn Peak

Summary of hike: Daly Creek is the northernmost drainage in Yellowstone National Park. The hike makes a gradual ascent up the scenic valley, crossing the rolling meadows and open hillsides parallel to Daly Creek. The hillsides are fringed with aspens and Douglas firs. The impressive Crown Butte, Lava Butte and King Butte formations are prominent throughout the hike. To the northeast is the Sky Rim Ridge.

Driving directions: From West Yellowstone, drive 31.4 miles north on Highway 191 (towards Bozeman) to the signed trail on the right between mile markers 30 and 31. Turn right and park in the lot.

From Big Sky, take Highway 191 south for 17.6 miles to the trailhead on the left.

Hiking directions: Head northeast, skirting around the right side of the embankment parallel to Daly Creek. At a quarter mile, cross the log footbridge over Daly Creek. To the north, outside the Yellowstone Park boundary, is the Crown Butte formation. King Butte rises high in the northeast. Climb the rolling ridge along the east side of the drainage through stands of lodgepole pines. Watch for a vernal pool on the right. At one mile, the trail climbs a small hill and crosses a couple of streams to a great profile view of Crown Butte, now to the west. Continue through the open meadows past a signed junction with the Black Butte Cutoff Trail on the right at 1.8 miles. The well-defined trail reaches the Tepee Creek Cutoff Trail junction at 2.6 miles. Though the trail continues, this is a good place to begin retracing your steps.

To hike further there are two options. To the north, the trail heads up three miles further to Daly Pass at the park's northern boundary on Sky Rim Ridge. The left fork heads west into the Tepee Creek valley (Hikes 42 and 43).

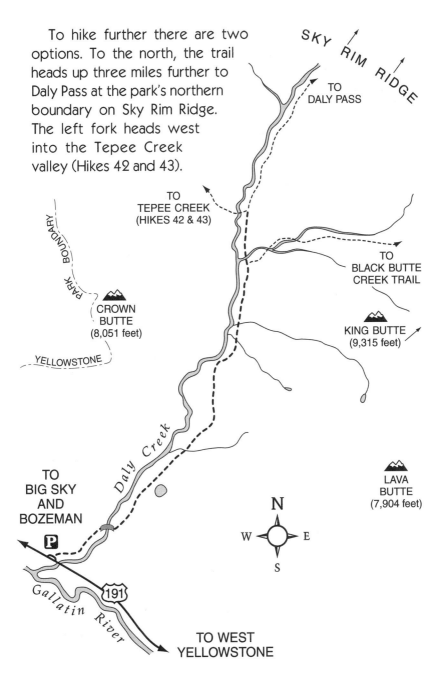

SKY RIM RIDGE

TO DALY PASS

TO TEPEE CREEK (HIKES 42 & 43)

TO BLACK BUTTE CREEK TRAIL

PARK BOUNDARY

CROWN BUTTE (8,051 feet)

KING BUTTE (9,315 feet)

YELLOWSTONE

Daly Creek

TO BIG SKY AND BOZEMAN

LAVA BUTTE (7,904 feet)

N
W · E
S

P

Gallatin River

191

TO WEST YELLOWSTONE

DALY CREEK TRAIL

Hike 45
Black Butte Creek Trail

Hiking distance: 4 miles round trip
Hiking time: 2 hours
Elevation gain: 600 feet
Maps: Trails Illustrated Mammoth Hot Springs
U.S.G.S. Big Horn Peak

Summary of hike: The Black Butte Creek Trail begins just northwest of Black Butte. The trail parallels Black Butte Creek up a beautiful forested drainage to a meadow at the base of King Butte. The narrow valley has aspen, lodgepole pine and Douglas fir. This trail is an access route up to Big Horn Peak, Shelf Lake and the summit of Sheep Mountain.

Driving directions: From West Yellowstone, drive 29.8 miles north on Highway 191 towards Bozeman, to the signed trail on the right, between mile markers 28 and 29. Park in the parking area on the left, 50 yards south of the signed trail.

From Big Sky, take Highway 191 south for 19.2 miles to the parking area on the right.

Hiking directions: Cross the highway to the signed trail on the north edge of Black Butte Creek. Hike up the forested draw between Black Butte and Lava Butte. Head gradually uphill, following the creek through meadows and pine groves along the creek drainage. Meander across the various slopes and rolling hills while remaining close to Black Butte Creek. At 1.5 miles, the trail enters a dense, old growth lodgepole forest. After a quarter-mile, the path breaks out into an open meadow. King Butte and Big Horn Peak tower above to the northeast. At two miles in the meadow at the base of King Butte is a signed trail junction. This is the turnaround spot.

To hike further, the left fork leads 2.1 miles to Daly Creek (Hike 44). The right fork crosses the meadow along Black Butte Creek. After crossing the creek, the trail begins a steep ascent to the summit of Bighorn Peak and on to Shelf Lake.

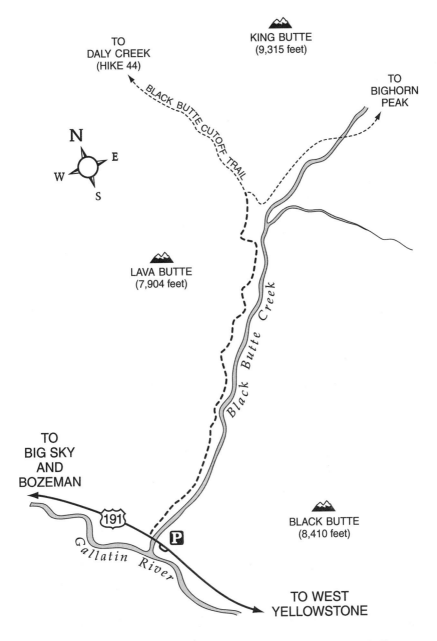

BLACK BUTTE CREEK TRAIL

Hike 46
Specimen Creek Trail

Hiking distance: 4.2 miles round trip
Hiking time: 2 hours
Elevation gain: 240 feet
Maps: Trails Illustrated Mammoth Hot Springs
U.S.G.S. Big Horn Peak

Summary of hike: The nearly flat Specimen Creek Trail follows Specimen Creek up the canyon through a mature forest dominated by lodgepole pines. This beautiful drainage crosses bridges over feeder streams to an open meadow at the confluence of the North Fork and East Fork of Specimen Creek. The meadow is frequented by elk and moose.

Driving directions: From West Yellowstone, drive 27.5 miles north on Highway 191 (towards Bozeman) to the signed trail on the right between mile markers 26 and 27. Turn right and park by the trailhead 30 yards ahead.
From Big Sky, take Highway 191 south for 21.5 miles to the trailhead on the left.

Hiking directions: Head east parallel to Specimen Creek through the lodgepole pine forest. Pass talus slopes on the northern side of the narrow drainage. As the canyon widens, the trail alternates between lush stands of pines and open meadows. At 1.3 miles cross a footbridge over a stream. Traverse the forested hillside to another footbridge over a stream to a signed trail split at two miles. The right fork follows the Sportsman Lake Trail to High Lake and Sportsman Lake, 6 and 8 miles ahead. Take the Specimen Creek Trail to the left. Within minutes is Campsite WE1. The campsite sits in an open meadow by Specimen Creek, meandering through the meadow. A short distance ahead is the confluence of the North Fork and the East Fork. This is our turnaround spot.
To hike further, the trail continues up to the headwaters of the North Fork at Crescent Lake and Shelf Lake.

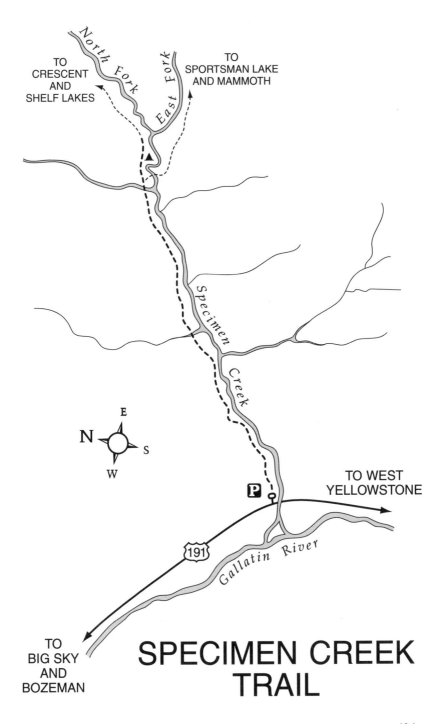

TO
CRESCENT
AND
SHELF LAKES

North Fork

East Fork

TO
SPORTSMAN LAKE
AND MAMMOTH

Specimen Creek

E

N ☩ S

W

TO WEST
YELLOWSTONE

P

191

Gallatin River

TO
BIG SKY
AND
BOZEMAN

SPECIMEN CREEK
TRAIL

Hike 47
Bacon Rind Creek Trail

Hiking distance: 4.2 miles round trip
Hiking time: 2 hours
Elevation gain: 200 feet
Maps: Trails Illustrated Mammoth Hot Springs
U.S.G.S. Divide Lake

Summary of hike: The Bacon Rind Creek Trail is the only hike inside Yellowstone that heads west from the Gallatin Valley. The flat easy trail parallels the meandering Bacon Rind Creek through a valley surrounded by high mountain peaks. Moose, elk and grizzly bears frequent the meadow. Beyond the western park boundary, the trail enters the Lee Metcalf Wilderness in the Gallatin National Forest.

Driving directions: From West Yellowstone, drive 23.5 miles north on Highway 191 (towards Bozeman) to the trailhead sign on the left between mile markers 22 and 23. Turn left on the unpaved road, and drive 0.3 miles to the trailhead parking area.

From Big Sky, take Highway 191 south for 25.5 miles to the trailhead turnoff on the right.

Hiking directions: Head south past the trail sign along the north side of Bacon Rind Creek. Follow the drainage upstream through beautiful stands of pines and firs. The path remains close to the riparian watercourse for the first 0.7 miles, where the valley opens up to the Gallatin River. Bacon Rind Creek flows placidly through the wide valley between the forested hillsides. Continue up the draw to the head of the valley and cross a stream. Evergreens enclose the top of the meadow at the signed Yellowstone National Park boundary. This is a good stopping place. To return, reverse route.

To hike further, the trail enters the Lee Metcalf Wilderness, crosses Migration Creek and ascends Monument Mountain.

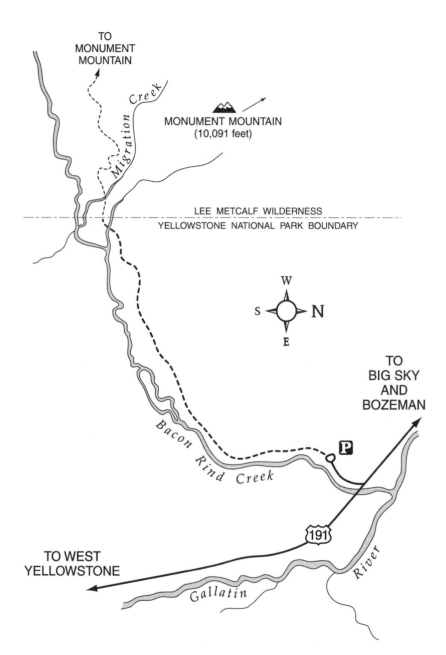

TO
MONUMENT
MOUNTAIN

Migration Creek

MONUMENT MOUNTAIN
(10,091 feet)

LEE METCALF WILDERNESS
YELLOWSTONE NATIONAL PARK BOUNDARY

W
S ◆ N
E

TO
BIG SKY
AND
BOZEMAN

Bacon Rind Creek

P

191

TO WEST
YELLOWSTONE

Gallatin River

BACON RIND CREEK TRAIL

Hike 48
Fawn Pass Trail to Fan Creek

Hiking distance: 3 miles round trip
Hiking time: 1.5 hours
Elevation gain: 200 feet
Maps: Trails Illustrated Mammoth Hot Springs
U.S.G.S. Divide Lake

Summary of hike: The Fawn Pass Trail to Fan Creek is an easy hike through forested rolling hills and scenic meadows. The Fan Creek Trail (not shown on the U.S.G.S. map) is a newer fishing access trail established in the early 1980s. From the junction with the Fawn Pass Trail, the Fan Creek Trail heads northeast along the creek through Fan Creek meadow. Moose and elk frequent this beautiful meadow.

Driving directions: From West Yellowstone, drive 22.8 miles north on Highway 191 (towards Bozeman) to the signed trail on the right, just south of mile marker 22. Turn right and park in the trailhead parking area.

From Big Sky, take Highway 191 south for 26.2 miles to the trailhead on the left.

Hiking directions: Head east down a short flight of steps on the Fawn Pass Trail. After the trail register, cross the meadow marbled with meandering streams that make up the upper Gallatin River. A series of wooden footbridges cross the various lucid streams. Ascend the slope and enter the forested hillside. Cross the gentle rolling hills to a signed trail split at 1.4 miles. The Fawn Pass Trail bears right to the Bighorn Pass Cutoff Trail and Fawn Pass. Take the Fan Creek Trail to the left. The trail descends into the wide open meadow to Fan Creek. At the creek is a wonderful picnic spot and place to rest.

To hike further, the trail follows Fan Creek through the mountain valley to the Sportsman Lake Trail, wading across Fan Creek three times.

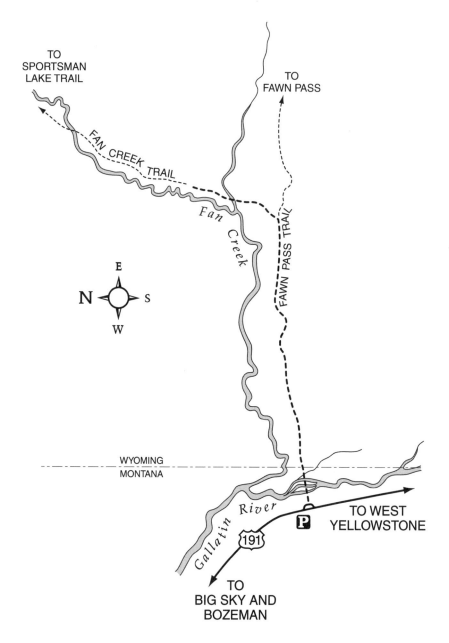

TO
SPORTSMAN
LAKE TRAIL

TO
FAWN PASS

FAN CREEK TRAIL

Fan Creek

FAWN PASS TRAIL

E
N S
W

WYOMING
MONTANA

Gallatin River

191

P

TO WEST
YELLOWSTONE

TO
BIG SKY AND
BOZEMAN

FAWN PASS TRAIL
TO FAN CREEK

Hike 49
Bighorn Pass Trail
along the Upper Gallatin River

Hiking distance: 1 to 12 miles round trip
Hiking time: Variable
Elevation gain: 150 feet
Maps: Trails Illustrated Mammoth Hot Springs
U.S.G.S. Divide Lake and Joseph Peak

Summary of hike: The Upper Gallatin Valley is a vast, open meadow that meanders along the Upper Gallatin River for many miles. This gives you the option of choosing your own distance. The relaxing hike through the scenic, treeless valley offers excellent trout fishing and wildlife viewing. The trail eventually leads over Bighorn Pass, which can be seen looming in the distance at the end of the valley.

Driving directions: From West Yellowstone, drive 21.3 miles north on Highway 191 (towards Bozeman) to the signed trail on the right between mile markers 20 and 21. Turn right and drive 0.2 miles to the parking area.

From Big Sky, take Highway 191 south for 27.7 miles to the trailhead on the left.

Hiking directions: The trail leads southeast past the hitching posts and trail sign along the west edge of the Gallatin River. Walk through the stands of lodgepole pines, heading upstream along the winding river. At a quarter mile, cross the log bridge over the river. After crossing, the trail continues southeast on the well-defined path. Follow the river through the broad grassy meadows, and enjoy spectacular views of the Gallatin Valley stretching to the east. You may turn around at any point along the trail. Bighorn Pass is 12 miles from the trailhead.

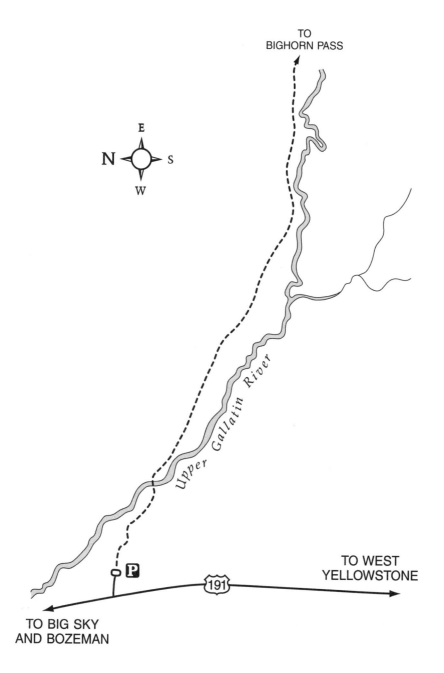

TO
BIGHORN PASS

E
N — S
W

Upper Gallatin River

TO WEST
YELLOWSTONE

P

191

TO BIG SKY
AND BOZEMAN

BIG HORN PASS TRAIL

Hike 50
Gneiss Creek Trail
from the Gallatin

Hiking distance: 3.6 miles round trip
Hiking time: 2 hours
Elevation gain: 300 feet
Maps: Trails Illustrated Mammoth Hot Springs
U.S.G.S. Richards Creek

Summary of hike: This hike follows the first portion of the Gneiss Creek Trail from the northwest trailhead in the Gallatin. The 14-mile trail leads through the Madison Valley, crossing several creeks en route to the southern trailhead at the Madison River Bridge (Hike 41). This hike is an easy walk through the beautiful open terrain to Campanula Creek, a tributary of Gneiss Creek. The valley is abundant with wildlife.

Driving directions: From West Yellowstone, drive 10.6 miles north on Highway 191 (towards Bozeman) to the signed trail on the right between mile markers 9 and 10. It is by the Fir Ridge Cemetery. Turn right and park in the parking area.

From Big Sky, take Highway 191 south for 38.4 miles to the trailhead on the left.

Hiking directions: Follow the old, grassy two-track road east through aspen and pine groves. Cross a small rise and parallel the signed Yellowstone Park boundary. At 0.3 miles, the trail enters the park at a sign-in register. Continue along the ridge above Duck Creek and Richards Creek to the south. Head east along the rolling hills spotted with pines and aspens. The trail gradually loses elevation past the forested slopes of Sandy Butte to the right. At the east end of Sandy Butte, descend into the draw to Campanula Creek. Follow the creek upstream a short distance to the creek crossing, the turnaround point for this hike. Return along the same path.

To hike further, cross the creek and continue southeast through the open, flat valley along Gneiss Creek.

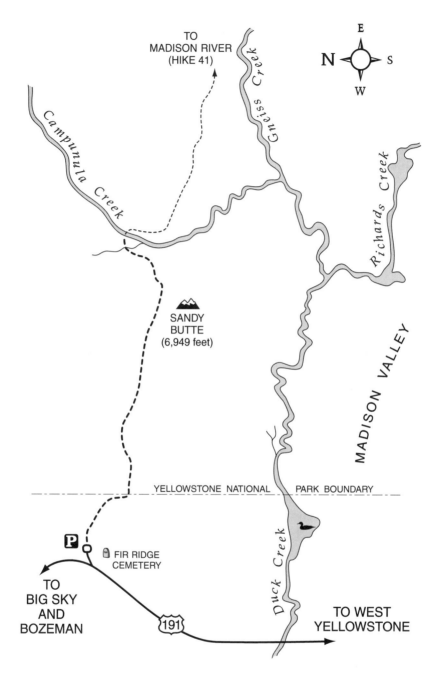

GNEISS CREEK TRAIL

Hike 51
Red Canyon Trail

Hiking distance: 2 miles round trip
Hiking time: 1 hour
Elevation gain: 500 feet
Maps: Madison and Gallatin Rivers Fishing and Hunting map
U.S.G.S. Mount Hebgen

Summary of hike: The Red Canyon Trail leads to the Cabin Creek Wildlife Management Area of the Lee Metcalf Wilderness. The trail follows Red Canyon Creek past the Red Canyon Fault, a 20-foot break on the southern slopes of Kirkwood Ridge. The fault was created in 1959 during the Madison River Canyon earthquake. Near the Kirkwood Ridge, there are scenic views back down the canyon.

Driving directions: From downtown West Yellowstone, drive 8 miles north on Highway 191 towards Bozeman. Turn left on Highway 287 towards Ennis. At 4.6 miles, turn right onto Red Canyon Road. This turn is marked with a Forest Service sign. Drive up Red Canyon Road 2.7 miles to the trailhead at the road's end and park.

Hiking directions: Head north on the well-defined path along the west side of Red Canyon Creek through a forest of lodgepole pine and Engelmann spruce. The prominent Kirkwood Ridge, with its sculpted limestone formations, towers above the trail to the northwest. At a quarter mile is a trail split. The right fork leads a short distance to the Red Canyon Fault. The main trail follows the left fork and ascends the hillside out of the lush drainage. Switchbacks lead up and across the open forest along the faultline. Continue gently up the draw, reaching a large wildflower-covered rolling meadow at one mile. There are great views back down Red Canyon to Hebgen Lake. This is the turnaround spot.

To hike further, the trail climbs alongside Red Canyon Creek to a junction with the Tepee Creek Trail.

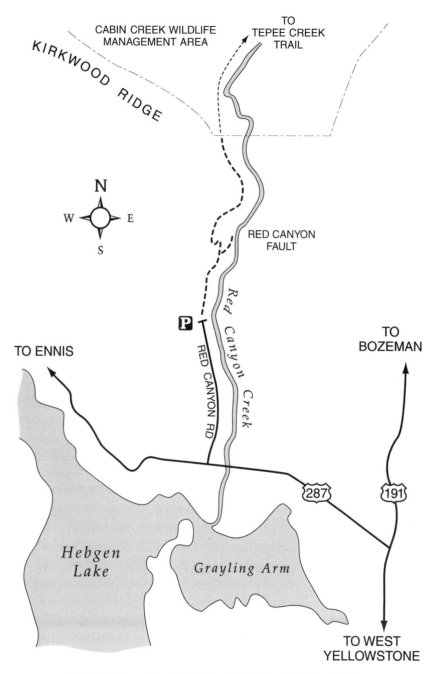

CABIN CREEK WILDLIFE
MANAGEMENT AREA

TO
TEPEE CREEK
TRAIL

KIRKWOOD RIDGE

N
W E
S

RED CANYON
FAULT

Red Canyon Creek

P

RED CANYON RD

TO ENNIS

TO
BOZEMAN

287

191

Hebgen
Lake

Grayling Arm

TO WEST
YELLOWSTONE

RED CANYON TRAIL

Hike 52
Horse Butte Lookout

Hiking distance: 3.4 miles round trip
Hiking time: 2 hours
Elevation gain: 500 feet
Maps: Madison and Gallatin Rivers Fishing and Hunting map
U.S.G.S. Madison Arm and Mount Hebgen

Summary of hike: The Horse Butte Lookout is a Forest Service fire tower. The uphill trail is an unpaved road that leads through open meadows that are often covered with wildflowers and an old growth Douglas fir forest. From 450 feet above the lake are views of the Madison Arm, Hebgen Lake, Edwards Peninsula, Yellowstone National Park and the Continental Divide. It is an excellent spot to view birds, including bald eagles, osprey and pelicans.

Driving directions: From downtown West Yellowstone, drive 5 miles north on Highway 191 towards Bozeman. Turn left at Rainbow Point Road. Turn left again 3.2 miles ahead at a four-way junction. Continue 1.6 miles to Horse Butte Lookout Road. The road, which is marked, forks to the right. This lightly used vehicle road is the hiking trail. Park anywhere along the side of the road.

Hiking directions: Hike northwest, curving up the unpaved road. With the continuous elevation gain, views open up of Hebgen Lake and the Madison Arm. At 1.3 miles the trail enters an old growth forest for a quarter mile. At the top, the trail curves around the hilltop meadow to the fire lookout and picnic area. It is a great place to have lunch and marvel at the beautiful views. Return along the same route.

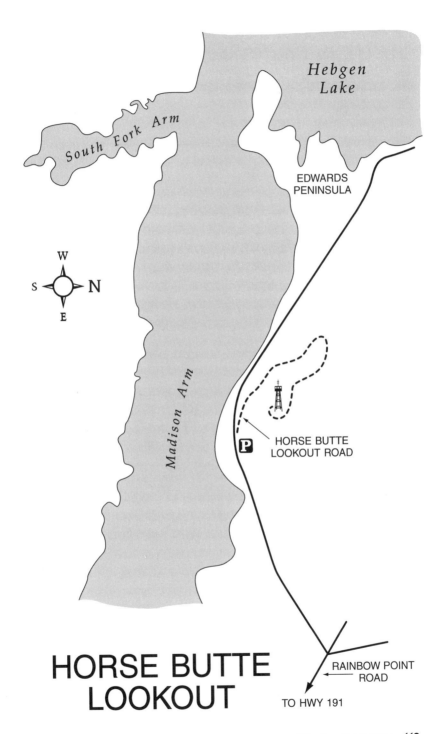

Hebgen Lake

South Fork Arm

EDWARDS PENINSULA

W
S · N
E

Madison Arm

P HORSE BUTTE
LOOKOUT ROAD

HORSE BUTTE
LOOKOUT

RAINBOW POINT
ROAD

TO HWY 191

Hike 53
Riverside Trail

Hiking distance: 3 miles round trip
Hiking time: 1.5 hours
Elevation gain: Level
Maps: Trails Illustrated Old Faithful
U.S.G.S. West Yellowstone

Summary of hike: The Riverside Trail is an easy river stroll along the banks of the Madison River. The trail begins in the town of West Yellowstone and follows a beautiful forested path into Yellowstone National Park. Primarily used as an angler and game trail, the path along the Madison River meanders across wildflower-covered meadows. In the morning, it is common to see moose along the river banks. During the winter, it is a popular cross-country ski trail.

Driving directions: In West Yellowstone, drive to the intersection of Madison Avenue and Boundary Street. These streets cross two blocks east of downtown. Park along Boundary Street.

A second access to the Madison River is located a half mile inside Yellowstone from the west entrance station. A one-mile road leads northeast to a parking area.

Hiking directions: From the east side of Boundary Street, walk through the opening in the pole fence. The fence is the west boundary of Yellowstone National Park. Head east through the forest for one mile, reaching an old gravel service road. The road descends to the banks of the Madison River. The trail meanders in both directions along the river. To the right (south) the trail leads to the West Entrance Road. To the left (north) the trail heads downstream across meadows to dense willow thickets. Return on the same trail back to your car.

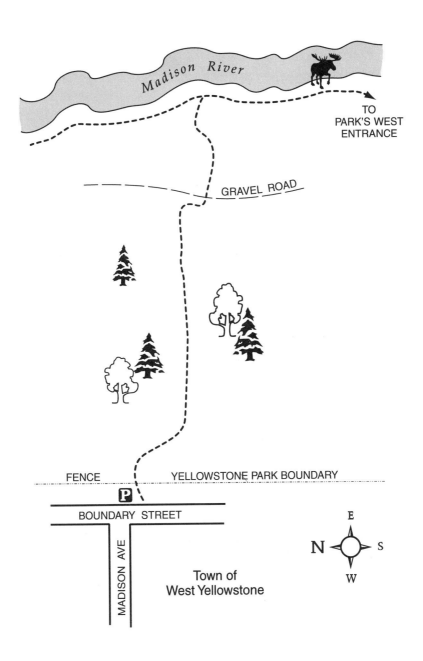

Madison River

TO
PARK'S WEST
ENTRANCE

GRAVEL ROAD

FENCE   YELLOWSTONE PARK BOUNDARY

P

BOUNDARY STREET

MADISON AVE

Town of
West Yellowstone

N · E · S · W

RIVERSIDE TRAIL

Hike 54
Targhee Creek Trail

Hiking distance: 5 miles round trip
Hiking time: 2.5 hours
Elevation gain: 250 feet
Maps: U.S.F.S. Gallatin National Forest—West Half
       Madison and Gallatin Rivers Fishing and Hunting map
       U.S.G.S. Targhee Pass and Targhee Peak, Idaho

Summary of hike: The Targhee Creek Trail parallels Targhee Creek to alpine Clark and Edwards Lakes near the headwaters of Targhee Creek. The trail follows the drainage between Targhee Peak to the west and Bald Peak to the east before joining the Continental Divide Trail. This hike meanders up the first 2.5 miles of the canyon along Targhee Creek through meadows and pine forests. Throughout the hike, Targhee Peak rises like a monolith high above the trail.

Driving directions: From downtown West Yellowstone, drive 11.4 miles on Highway 20 towards Idaho. Turn right at the Targhee Creek Trails. There is a sign on the highway marking the turn. Drive one mile to the well-marked trailhead and park.

Hiking directions: From the parking area, head north past the trail sign towards the prominent Targhee Peak. The trail strolls gently up the drainage through pine forests, open hillsides and rolling meadows. At 2.5 miles a footbridge crosses over to the west side of Targhee Creek. This is our turnaround spot.

To hike further, the trail continues up the canyon, reaching Clark Lake at 6.5 miles while gaining an additional 1,800 feet in elevation.

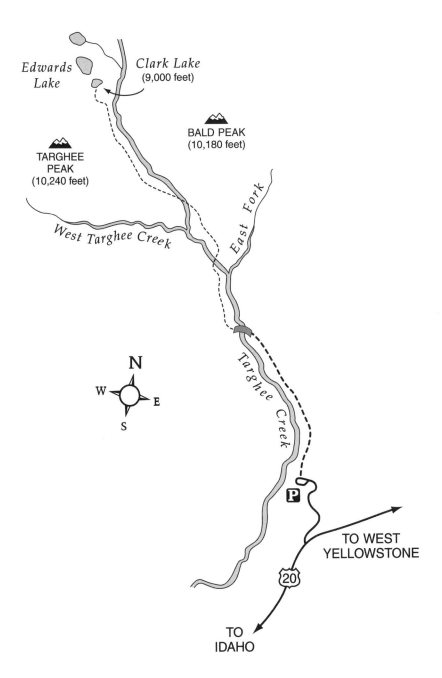

Edwards
Lake

Clark Lake
(9,000 feet)

BALD PEAK
(10,180 feet)

TARGHEE
PEAK
(10,240 feet)

West Targhee Creek

East Fork

Targhee Creek

N
W E
S

P

TO WEST
YELLOWSTONE

20

TO
IDAHO

TARGHEE CREEK TRAIL

Other Day Hike Guidebooks

Day Hikes on the California Central Coast 14.95

Day Hikes Around Monterey and Carmel, California 14.95

Day Hikes in San Luis Obispo County, California 14.95

Day Hikes Around Santa Barbara, California. 11.95

Day Hikes in Ventura County, California 11.95

Day Hikes in Sequoia and Kings Canyon National Parks 12.95

Day Hikes in Yosemite National Park. 11.95

Day Hikes Around Lake Tahoe 8.95

Day Hikes Around Los Angeles. 11.95

Day Hikes in Sedona, Arizona 9.95

Day Hikes in Yellowstone National Park 9.95

Day Hikes in Grand Teton National Park and Jackson Hole. 8.95

Day Hikes in the Beartooth Mountains
Red Lodge, Montana to Yellowstone National Park 11.95

Day Hikes Around Bozeman, Montana 11.95

Day Hikes Around Missoula, Montana 11.95

Day Hikes on Oahu 11.95

Day Hikes on Maui 11.95

Day Hikes on Kauai 11.95

Day Trips on St. Martin. 9.95

These books may be purchased at your local bookstore or
outdoor shop. Or, order them direct from the distributor:

The Globe Pequot Press
246 Goose Lane · P.O. Box 480 · Guilford, CT 06437-0480
www.globe-pequot.com

800-243-0495

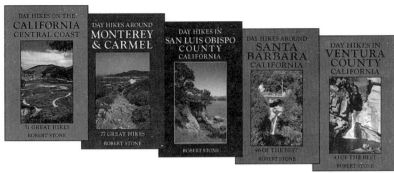

DAY HIKES ON THE **CALIFORNIA** CENTRAL COAST — 71 GREAT HIKES — ROBERT STONE

DAY HIKES AROUND **MONTEREY & CARMEL** — 77 GREAT HIKES — ROBERT STONE

DAY HIKES IN **SAN LUIS OBISPO COUNTY** CALIFORNIA — ROBERT STONE

DAY HIKES AROUND **SANTA BARBARA** CALIFORNIA — 46 OF THE BEST — ROBERT STONE

DAY HIKES IN **VENTURA COUNTY** CALIFORNIA — 43 OF THE BEST — ROBERT STONE

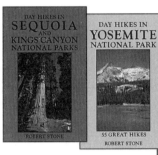

DAY HIKES IN **SEQUOIA** AND **KINGS CANYON** NATIONAL PARKS — ROBERT STONE

DAY HIKES IN **YOSEMITE** NATIONAL PARK — 55 GREAT HIKES — ROBERT STONE

DAY HIKES AROUND **LAKE TAHOE** — ROBERT STONE

DAY HIKES AROUND **LOS ANGELES** — 45 GREAT HIKES — ROBERT STONE

DAY HIKES IN **SEDONA** ARIZONA — 25 FAVORITE HIKES — ROBERT STONE

DAY HIKES IN **YELLOWSTONE** NATIONAL PARK — 54 GREAT HIKES — ROBERT STONE

DAY HIKES IN **GRAND TETON** NATIONAL PARK AND **JACKSON HOLE** — ROBERT STONE

DAY HIKES IN THE **BEARTOOTH MOUNTAINS** — RED LODGE, MONTANA TO YELLOWSTONE NATIONAL PARK — ROBERT STONE

DAY HIKES AROUND **BOZEMAN** MONTANA — INCLUDING THE GALLATIN CANYON AND PARADISE VALLEY — ROBERT STONE

DAY HIKES AROUND **MISSOULA** MONTANA — INCLUDING THE BITTERROOTS AND THE SEELEY-SWAN VALLEY — ROBERT STONE

DAY HIKES ON **OAHU** — ROBERT STONE

DAY HIKES ON **MAUI** — ROBERT STONE

DAY HIKES ON **KAUAI** — ROBERT STONE

DAY TRIPS ON **ST. MARTIN** — ROBERT STONE

Notes